THE SHOE BURNIN'

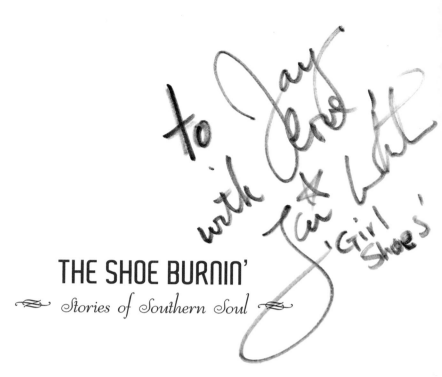

THE SHOE BURNIN'

~ *Stories of Southern Soul* ~

Edited by Joe Formichella

RIVER'S EDGE
— MEDIA —

LITTLE ROCK, ARKANSAS
2013

THE SHOE BURNIN' STORIES OF SOUTHERN SOUL
PUBLISHED BY RIVER'S EDGE MEDIA, LLC
100 MORGAN KEEGAN DRIVE, STE. 305
LITTLE ROCK, AR 72202

First Edition 2013.

"A Sin of Omission" was previously published in November 2009 by *Wildlife in North Carolina* magazine and is copyrighted by the N.C. Wildlife Resources Commission.

"All the Way to Memphis" was originally published in *Delta Blues*, edited by Carolyn Haines.

"Spastic" first appeared in *Arts and Letters*.

"Smash and Grab" was originally published in *Story Quarterly*, edited by M.M.M. Hayes.

"I Haven't Stopped Dancing Yet", a modified version, first appeared in *love, bourbon street*, edited by Greg Herren and Paul J. Willis.

Printed in the United States of America.

The Shoe Burnin' Stories of Southern Soul: a literary anthology
edited by Joe Formichella.
ISBN 13: 978-1-940595-00-9 (Hardback)

Acknowledgements

Thanks to David Martin, Kerry Brooks, Brent Gambill, Cary Smith, Jill Martin, Tyler Cobb, Paula Guajardo and all the fine folks at River's Edge Media for their vision and belief. An infinite amount of gratitude from all of us goes to our mad Dr. Frankenstein, Shari Smith, the architect of this loveable monster, as well as her muse, Jim Davis. A personal thank you, thank you, to Suzanne Hudson, for her crazy brilliant editorial eye, among other things, and to Jay Quayley for his vicious pencil. Thanks to all the contributors, of course, for the opportunity, and your patience.

Thank you Terry and Patrick, for your indomitable spirit and inspiration.

Contents

Introduction

So, just what the hell is a Shoe Burnin' anyway? Well, according to legend, on a cold winter's night somewhere near Brewton, Alabama, some years ago, some number of Brewton and East Brewton acquaintances were huddled around a hearth swapping stories, singing songs, when they ran out of firewood. Rather than brave the elements a trip to the wood pile would require, a box of old shoes materialized and fueled the fire for another hour or so. The first thing you have to know, if you haven't already guessed, is that there was alcohol involved. In fact, that may be the single aspect of this story that the so-called original shoe-burners can all agree on.

"We were sitting around drinking one night," they'll tell you, "and someone said, 'You know what we should do? We should go see Gary.'"

Gary Fuqua, notorious hermit, recluse, woods-dwelling good ol' boy.

It gets progressively fuzzy after that.

"When was that?" Cindy Sasser Sanders, one original, asks another, Suzanne Hudson. "'74, or '75?"

"I'm not sure. But you do remember, right?"

"I remember we brought some shoes."

"We did?"

See? There's no consensus about when. There isn't even total agreement about who was involved. Hudson, at one point, wonders, "Was I with Mike then, or Mack?" and then tries to mitigate the confusion by saying, "They sound the same."

"Linda was there, wasn't she?"

"I know Peter was there," Hudson says. She remembers this, explicitly, because at some point during the ensuing cow-paddy war—sorry, forgot to mention the cow-paddy war—Peter, upon hearing the "enemy's" approach, told her, "Get down! Pretend you're a turd."

Except Peter Goodwin can't confirm much of anything. "The shoe-burning?" he says. "I remember nothing at all about that except that I once attended such a thing," hardly registering on the continuum of proof, maybe satisfying an "air of reality," but nowhere near "beyond a reasonable doubt."

Given a little more time, though, he allows, "I take that back. There is one memory from the shoe-burning, and only one. That guy, Gary Fuqua, was sitting by the fire with an old yearbook, showing me some pictures of his classmates and generally reminiscing," presumably prior to chucking that into the fire as well. "After one anecdote about a class-mate I asked, 'So whatever happened to him?' Gary took a drag off his cigarette, then said matter-of-factly, 'He's a convict,' just as he might have said that he's a pharmacist or a salesman. That struck me as hilarious for some reason."

Still seeking verification, Suzanne asks Cindy, "You remember the war, right?" who only says after some consideration, "No… I remember there was all that land out there."

"But you remember Gary," Hudson says, getting a little desperate, "driving up a tree?"

"Yeah, yeah," she says, finally agreeing on something, "I remember the lights."

But we're getting ahead of ourselves.

Because any journalist, any good journalist—you've seen the mov-ies—would tell you not to go with a story until you have at least three reliable corroborative sources. Otherwise, there's a real good chance the story won't hold up, will be open to challenge. One source reduces the story to a binary dichotomy of "he said-she said", tit-for-tat, at the very best. Binary dichotomies are unstable, untrustworthy, even dan-gerous—if you consider the whole matter-anti-matter dilemma. A pair of sources—and only a pair—screams collusion, fabrication, a "great" idea hatched over beers one night in the absence of any other thing to talk about. But three, with three, you've got balance, stability, *veritas*. In a word: perfection. Hell, according to Arlo, you've got a movement!

But we don't have that luxury, can't hope for that level of comfort. We've got the Mayor's word—the Mayor of Waterhole Branch, that is.

We've got a handful of equivocating co-conspirators, who all vaguely remember an "original" shoe-burning, but that's about it. There was a night out at Gary's cabin, in the woods, near the pasture, nearly forty (or thirty-nine, or thirty-eight) years ago. There were stories, songs, and whiskey. While it was too inclement to go outside to replenish wood for the fireplace—besides, Gary happened to have a box full of orphaned shoes the other participants didn't hesitate at all pitching into the fire—it was somehow perfectly fine, a little later, to choose up sides and wage a middle-of-the-night, middle-of-nowhere cow-paddy war.

"It was me, and Peter, and Linda," Hudson says, "against you, and Mike…"

"Or Mack?"

And at some point, they ran out of whiskey.

"It was about three," the testimony follows, "'cause I remember saying, 'Gary, where are you going to get whiskey at three in the morning?'"

"Don't worry," Gary answered, again matter-of-factly, but then promptly drove his car up a tree, headlights illuminating the early morning sky like it was a Hollywood premiere.

"But Gary wasn't hurt," they always add.

So it goes.

The thing is, however much you do or don't believe any of the original shoe-burning miscreants, this story, all their stories, were never meant to be permanitized, captured between the covers of a book, were never meant to be part of any historical record. The whole event was organic—to use the current, and kindest jargon. It was a lark. The very notion of documenting the whole sordid affair didn't occur to anyone until after the tradition was revived some thirty-five (or thirty-two, or thirty-seven, for that matter) years later once a couple of them became neighbors on a swath of acreage at the end of a dirt road tucked against a tributary of Fish River in south Baldwin County, Alabama, known as Waterhole Branch.

Singer-songwriter Grayson Capps writes about the place as his heart in a tender verse. "Down a sandy lane," former Alabama poet laureate Sue Walker begins her "Mardi Gras Wedding," "just a moon pie's throw from Mobile, Alabama, a friend marries on the bayou…" Clearly the place is inspirational.

And the revival occurred much the same way as the original, sitting around one night, sipping whiskey, when someone says, "You know what we should do?"

Even at that, it remained an informal, Saturday-after-Thanksgiving excuse to burn shit, sing songs, laugh, and tell stories—good stories, mind you, stories about shoes that had trod everywhere from the D.C. Mall to the Parthenon, shoes that had pushed off the floorboard of a submerged automobile, skipped up and down the stairway to heaven, and danced the light fantastic. The shoe-burning didn't become the subject of an anthology until the maniacal collaboration of Shari Smith and Jim Davis and David Martin—scary geniuses, all of them—hatched through an email exchange and presented to the rest of this—what would you call them, exactly? An assemblage? The inmates? I can only allude to what Shari calls them, "Our f***ed-up little family"—this crowd in a way that would certainly do Gary proud. "You know what we should do…" We should collect some of the stories and anthologize them. After all, any pair of shoes has a story to tell. Some of the stories that follow have been thrown in the fire, and some have yet to be. "You know what we should do?" And with little more direction than that, we give you *The Shoe Burnin', Stories of Southern Soul.*

We don't have any actual convicts in this collection that I know of, though that might need to be further defined to be certain. Same with salesmen—but we're all, always selling something, aren't we?—and pharmacists—though self-medication could easily fall into that category, which renders us all guilty, again. Grayson, making it okay, writes that if he gets "the right medication," he'll join us there, at Waterhole Branch.

We do have journalists—three of them, in fact, but don't let that fool you. We've also got troubadours, singer-songwriters, seasoned writers, virgins, Grammy winners, Hackney winners, and poets—at least three—educators, a public servant—by fiat—even a tennis pro, which, on paper, ought to lend a little cachet to the project. In the end, though, what we've got is a pack of liars—albeit some are professional liars; that is, they make their living through their prevarications—storytellers who can't, and won't be held accountable for anything they tell you.

That's not to say, though, that it wasn't an enjoyable and educational endeavor. When a Nashville hit machine tells you—Strunk & White be damned—that it sounds better to his ear, you bend the rules. When the same entreaty—"Good story, now give it to me in your voice"—works with both a veteran writer and a novice, you begin to believe in process. And when you swing for the fences suggesting the engineer goddess write hers in character, and she rises to the occasion, and beyond, you suspect someone's sprinkling fairy dust over the whole project. Whether tutelage or magic, it's been a delightful learning curve, for me, certainly, for the writers, I hope, but most importantly, for you, dear reader. Enjoy.

Joe Formichella

BOOTS

by Ed Southern

What those college kids wore on their feet was their second amazement. Did they neither know nor imagine that this ground was thick with weapons of infection, with rusty nails and metal shards sharper than X-ACTO knives, with splinters and screws and broken glass?

And that was just in the ground, in the churned-up yards and the street; no one wearing shoes like those could wade sensibly into the wrecks and ruins and heaps of shambles in which they were there to work.

Yet they were come among it shod in nothing but old tennis shoes, or even—Jesus!—elaborate sandals, nothing but thin strips of rubber, canvas, or imitation leather between them and punctures, staph or lockjaw. Aaron and Jason realized that these college kids, in the run of their lives, never had a call for serious boots like Aaron's Red Wings or Jason's Justins, but that did not lessen their amazement. Did they think they'd float above this damage all about? Were they not intent on the task they'd volunteered to do?

Jason and Aaron talked about that second amazement that evening, after they'd worked till dusk. They sat in plastic chairs, outside the cheap room they'd found in an America's Best Value Inn, with a sack emptied of Krystal burgers and a five-dollar Styrofoam cooler full of ice and

Natty Light between them, smoking Camels. They looked out across the parking lot and the power lines and the highway, watching the traffic come and go and stop at the Exxon opposite them, the trucks and the cars rolling as if nothing were different than before. That sort of surprised them, as breathless as the cable news had been.

They talked about their second amazement, and how little the college kids seemed to know about anything useful like masonry or wiring or plumbing, until talk of flimsy shoes led to talk of flimsy clothes, and talk of flimsy clothes led to talk of female legs.

"You pick you out a pair yet?"

"Shit fire, son, that ain't what we're here for."

"Yeah, I knew you had. I saw you talking to her."

"Psssht. Hell." Aaron went inside the room to piss.

When he came back, Jason was holding out a can and saying, "No, but I'll give you a beer," to a man dressed in the rags of an Army jacket and polyester work pants. He wore flip-flops on his feet. His stink of rotten food and smoke, of having soiled himself, hit Aaron as he reached his chair.

The man took the can and raised it in a toast. "You a gentleman." He popped the tab and took a long draw. "Where you gentlemen from?"

"Rock Springs, North Carolina," Jason said.

"North Carolina. I been to Charlotte, North Carolina. Is Rock Springs close to Charlotte?"

"Closer than it used to be."

"I'll come visit next time I'm there. What brings you gentlemen to Birmingham?"

They answered him, sort of; they could have answered longer or shorter than they did, but they told him what they could and would. They told him what they wanted to tell, and what they thought he'd want to hear, the way anyone, anywhere, tells any kind of story, though maybe a little more so.

"Well," Jason said, "I mean, we saw all about it on the TV, like I guess everyone did. I finished up a rotation and went by Aaron's, and he said, 'You know, we'd be like a Dream Team for something like this.' So we were like, 'What the hell,' got in the truck and came on down."

Jason left a dawdling and plotless shift at the firehouse to find Aaron watching YouTube, image after image, twister after twister, rampage. They threw a few clothes into duffels and gathered what they thought were appropriate tools: bow saws, hacksaws, Jason's hand-me-down chain saw, sledgehammers, claw hammers, crowbars, shovels.

"My man here's a firefighting professional," Aaron said. "I'm just a lowly volunteer, but I'm EMT-certified, too. I'm apprenticing with a general contractor, so I know a little bit about everything to do with a house—the wiring, the plumbing . . ."

"So, yeah, we thought we could help out some down here."

They were not long back from the service, from the Sandbox, and it complicated their feelings about disaster in ways they had not yet noticed, much less put into words.

"We just got in his truck and drove," Aaron said. "I mean, we didn't know, like, where we were supposed to go to volunteer, who we should report to. We figured something this big, we'd figure it out."

They left on a Thursday evening. They drove through the night, crossing into Alabama at one in the morning, coming into a place called Irondale at two. They found a Wal-Mart and parked the truck and went inside to piss, and slept in the truck until after dawn.

"We just got lucky, and ran into a fella that was getting together some volunteers to clean up a few houses." They spent the morning wandering, until they stopped at a firehouse, where the firemen sent them to a clearinghouse, where they would have been brute force on a loading dock if a professor from a college had not noticed Aaron's Rock Springs V.F.D. T-shirt. The Professor was from North Carolina himself, once, and knew of Rock Springs. (They never did quite catch his name, so they just called him the Professor.) They told him how they were like a Dream Team for something like this, and he invited them to come with him and his crew of college students who'd volunteered. Aaron and Jason climbed back in Jason's truck and followed the Professor's car, and the line of his students' cars, through the city, north of the grid and the gray and the hollow industrial hulks, and over a ridge and onto a cul-de-sac carved into the sharp north-facing slope, half its houses ruined by the storm.

The man then asked, so they told him, no, they didn't know a soul in Birmingham; they just wanted to help.

The man raised his can in another toast. "Y'all is gentlemen." He offered them blessings and promised them prayers. He closed his eyes and raised his hands (and the beer) to God and prayed for them right then, asking the Lord to look down and bless these His servants for their goodness and kindness of heart in this, their time of need. He said Amen and drained the can. "Y'all sure you can't spare a dollar for me?"

Jason shook his head. "We weren't even sure we could get a room for the night."

"Alright. Shit. Y'all have a fine evening." He threw the empty into the bushes, and walked away along the highway. They watched until he left their view.

"You know he's just the second person down here who's asked where we're from?" Aaron said.

If anyone, then or later, had asked Aaron what he'd expected to find in Alabama in those days, he'd have shrugged. Probably he'd have said, "Me and Jason, we were like a Dream Team for that sort of thing." He had put little thought or imagination into what they'd find at the end of that long night drive; he had no experience to frame it by. He'd been a baby when Hurricane Hugo hit, and though he'd heard his mama's stories enough to believe sometimes that he remembered it, he couldn't really tell you what a natural disaster looked like. He knew that all the state wouldn't look like the land tore up on the cable news and YouTube, but those were the only images he carried to Alabama with him.

But if anyone had asked Aaron what he'd expected to find, and then held him down and not let up until he told the truth, he finally would have admitted, maybe even screamed, that he needed to do something good.

They were early to the cul-de-sac Saturday morning, staying as they were so close to the interstate, and being there for no stated purpose than to help, and feeling no need for orientation or campus meet-up. The motel's free coffee was still warm in the cups in their hands, and biscuit crumbs fell from their Carhartts when they stepped out of the truck and into the risen sun and the silence.

They could point to piles of debris they'd helped to heap at the curbs. They could identify the jagged gutters and trim that Aaron had wrenched and pried from the house before they fell, and the logs that Jason had cut with his chainsaw to reduce the fallen trees into manageable parts. They could walk freely around back yards that yesterday had been choked with ruin. But for all that they could do, when they stood by the truck and looked around in a sweep, took in the totality of the cul-de-sac and the scar that ran across the ridgeline, they could not see as how they'd made a scratch, a ding, a dent in the comprehensive finish of the destruction.

That had been their first amazement. Gaping and bating their breath, they'd stepped from the truck and stared at the line, the scar, at its precision, the demarcation that came so clearly to the eye. On the hillside above they could see, with no effort, where the tornado came over the crest and raced downhill to pass where they stood; turning, they could see where it raced on and down through the pines, and up the subsequent ridge, and on. All inside that line was broken; the ground itself was churned. On the cul-de-sac, the houses standing to either side of the line still stood, maybe mussed, but no more than after a rager or a simple thunderstorm. Next door, the houses inside the line now lay—heaped, or half-eaten, or de-constituted into building materials, hurled and spread about like the toys of a spoiled and angry child.

Aaron and Jason had seen houses—houses here, Stateside, American homes, secure and well-built—destroyed. They had watched them burn before their eyes and despite their best work. They'd seen the walls collapse around them while they raced the fire to get out. They'd torn down houses themselves, wiped them stud by joist from the earth, so they would neither fall on some poor soul nor impede new construction. Soon, then, that Friday, Jason and Aaron had stopped gaping, breathed as usual, and almost felt at home. First they'd had to admit their amazement that wind, not fire, that nothing but common air, had done all this.

Saturday morning they had to do it again, admit and process their amazement, break it down and discard every element but one, before they could get to work.

Before long the cul-de-sac crawled, being a Saturday, with volunteers. Many wore matching shirts, advertising their church or school or civic club, and they segregated themselves by worksite. Each group had signed on for, and attached themselves to, one or more street numbers, and those lots were theirs, and no other's. Jason and Aaron stuck to the yard they'd left the day before, and watched the yards around them fill.

Minivans and SUVs parked and let out Boy Scouts and Sunday school classes, even a corporate staff. A bus belonging to a well-publicized international ministry pulled up across the street.

Jason with his chainsaw went after another tree, a tulip poplar fallen across the back of the lot, so the college boys would have something to do when they arrived. The tree had been old, so the boughs were thick and took a long time to saw through; once sawn, they fell to the earth with a deep, percussive whump. He sawed the boughs off, and then into logs that could be barrowed or carried, until the only boughs left on the tree were those the trunk rested on. He was about to start on the trunk itself, at the skinny end that had been the top, when he heard another chainsaw whine. He looked next door and met the eyes of a sturdy, gray-haired man who'd taken his station by a fallen pine, a troop of teenage boys in line behind him. The man nodded and Jason nodded, and they went to work slicing the trees away.

Aaron, trusting to his Red Wings, entered what had been the house. He didn't need a door. With balance and care he ascended bricks, both fallen and standing, and stepped into the kitchen. Half the house's eastern wall lay crumbled on the grass; the other half was just gone, taken away. Aaron, the day before, had felt an old, silly shame at seeing so much of rooms into which he'd never been invited, whose owners he did not know or see or know to be alive; the sight made him feel like a thief, as it had before, and it made him feel sick to feel that way again. This time he stepped into that room, that kitchen, with balance and care, feeling the floorboards before he gave them his weight. Whoever lived here, or had, loved Jesus, or had. Jesus, and decorative salt-and-pepper shakers. Small pieces of ceramic or plastic or glass, molded and perfo-rated on top, sat unmoved and ignorant where they'd sat for years, on pressboard shelves nailed to the wood-paneled interior walls. This house stood half-naked to Aaron, to all the world. Yesterday their mattress had lain sodden in the street; they had seen the sheets on which these people had slept. Aaron stepped from the kitchen into the den.

He was trying to find the source of the stench. Yesterday, as they'd worked their way through the scattered debris closer to the house itself, a foul smell of decomposition rose to them. It could have been sewage; it could have been a varmint; it could have been a pet. It could have been some fabric, waterlogged and rotting from exposure. Aaron did not relish the search, much less the prospect of success, but he knew he could handle it, and he knew it was something he could do to spare the others. He knew he had smelled worse smells from worse sources. He felt sure they had not.

He was intent and heard a man holler "Hey," and holler some more, before he thought the hollering might be at him. A big man, so bearded and sunglassed he might not have had a face, stood in the street.

"You're not supposed to be in there," he hollered at Aaron.

Aaron nodded. "I'll be alright."

"You ain't supposed to be in there."

"I ain't just hanging out. I'll be out before long."

"You need to come on out of there now."

Aaron stopped, planted his feet shoulder-width apart, straightened his legs and his spine to reach his full height, and turned to face the man full-on. His hands hung at his sides, the fingers curled halfway to fists, his shoulders back and squared.

"You need," he said, "to find someone else to be an asshole to."

The man stared, or Aaron guessed he was staring, behind the sunglasses.

"I'm trying to do a job here," Aaron said, "a job I don't see you or anybody else stepping up to do, and I'll be . . ."

The man didn't wait for Aaron to finish, didn't bother listening. He threw up an arm in something like dismissal and shouted, "Fine, you little punk, bust your ass and see if I care," as he walked to the yard next door. Aaron watched him walk away and stood, still, for a long moment, seething and ashamed.

Volunteers continued to come onto the cul-de-sac and the streets around it, cars and pickup trucks covering the curbs, their windows and bumpers demanding that God bless America. The Professor arrived, and the college kids, some new, some of the same, almost all of them ill-shod again. She did not come, the long-haired, coltish girl Aaron had talked to yesterday. He saw that he did not see her, and wondered if he was why.

"Hey," the Professor called out to him. "Good morning. Glad to see you back." He came to the edge of the pile that had been the east wall, checking the ground where he set his feet like he was toeing a mark.

"Um, Aaron, hey, when they assigned us this site they told us not to go into the house itself. It's a liability issue."

"It'll be alright. I've done this a million times," Aaron said. "In houses in even worse shape than this one."

"Oh, I'm sure you have and all, but still."

"I'm just trying to find what's making that stink. It might be a health hazard for all of us."

"Oh. Yeah, I hadn't thought about that. Okay. Just, please, be careful."

"I will. And I won't loot nothing, neither."

With balance and care Aaron stepped toward the back of the house, toward the bedrooms and the space where the stairs had gone down to the basement. The back of the house was a crumble and a ruin, the basement become a catchpond for the cinder blocks and shingles. Aaron sniffed and tried to follow his nose, but the stench was faint and shifting in the early-morning cool. He was pretty sure the smell came from where the basement had been, from underneath the pile, where anything that lived and had any sense would have gone and been when the tornado struck above. He was pretty sure he could get to it, though he'd have to move a few dozen blocks and parts of blocks, and whole clouds of pink insulation, and nail-studded beams, and what looked to be a navy blue three-piece suit, and a few floral-print church-going dresses, and a brown teddy bear.

He was pretty sure he could get down there, could pick his way across and down the pile, down to, and then below, the level of the earth. He crouched at the lip, creaking the last load-bearing floorboard, and considered his possible paths.

Don't wonder if they lived or died, he told himself. You know, you know, it don't do a bit of good. You know it'll only drive you crazy. Don't wonder. Don't ask nobody. Don't mind and don't care.

He stood, shifted to his left, and reached out his foot to a block that seemed stuck fast and stable. It was as it seemed, but few others were as he descended. They teetered with his step, tossing the foot that held his weight to and fro. He still was young and his joints were limber, and even in his heavy Red Wings he could let his bones and muscles move as they needed to keep him upright. When he steadied, he continued. When he felt like he was close, he took his gloves from his hip pocket and worked his hands into them, pulling the Velcro straps tight around his wrists. He knelt and took hold of a cinder block, and flung it from him. Then another; more.

Jason sawed the last reasonable length from the tulip poplar's trunk and let go of the chainsaw's trigger, a tiny bit enchanted, as always, by the motor's soft decline. As it eased he began to hear the Professor yelling—behind him, up toward the street—and he turned to look.

The Professor had raised one arm to the remains of the house, like some kind of ancient salute, and waved it every now and then. "Whoa—hey!" he shouted. "Hey! Whoa! You can't do that! We're not supposed to be doing that!"

Jason followed the Professor's line of vision. He saw all manner of debris fly through the air in crazed, inconsistent arcs—a sheet of tar paper jerking up and swaying down, the back of a wooden chair spinning on an axis as it traced a parabola. In the center of all the arcs somebody hunched, head down to the task, and Jason knew it would be Aaron before he saw that it was so.

Everyone in that yard, and in the yard next door, was looking at him. The Professor continued shouting from just beyond what had been walls. Jason set down his chainsaw and started toward him, and as he did he saw the sturdy man next door confer with a big, bearded man in sunglasses. They started toward him too.

"I told him he wasn't supposed to be in there," the bearded man said.

"Hey," the sturdy man shouted at Aaron, "you're gonna get yourself or somebody else hurt doing that."

"I told him he's not supposed to," the Professor said.

"Little punk thinks he knows better . . ."

"Y'all calm down and back off a sec," Jason said. He climbed into the house the same way Aaron had, and approached him from six o'clock, and started talking to him well before he was near him.

"Aaron, man, what you doing there, honcho?"

"Trying to find whatever's making that stink."

"Cool, man, that's a good idea. Well, hell, actually it might be a terrible idea, since personally I wouldn't want to lay eyes on whatever's making that kind of a smell.

"In fact, I think that idea sucks. I think that's about the damn stupidest idea you've ever had.

"And that's saying something.

"'Cause you've had some stupid ideas."

At last Aaron said, "Fuck you."

"Can I pull you away from your shitty idea long enough to help me with something?"

"What you need help with?"

"I want to start on something over here, and I don't think any of these college kids pack the gear for it.

"At least, I'd feel better if it was you working on it with me."

"Sure," Aaron said. He stood and looked at Jason. "What you wanting to start on?"

Jason looked back, at the limit of his imagination.

"What the fuck, man," Aaron said. He turned his back to Jason, hunkered down. "I got to find whatever it is that stinks so bad."

Jason stepped off the last load-bearing floorboard and skipped down the pile, with more quickness than care, to get to Aaron before he flung more of the house into the air.

"Buddy—shit!—Aaron, man, listen—fuck!—Aaron." He reached his friend and held onto his shoulders, as if he had caught himself from falling. He spoke just above a whisper into his ear. "Everybody's looking. They're all having a shit-fit over this. They're all looking over here at you like you've snapped, and pretty soon they're going to start whispering about PTSD or some shit."

Aaron turned, and his grin scared Jason, but only a very little. "I ain't snapped."

"I know it, but they don't."

"So? Screw them." Aaron looked at the three men standing at parade rest beside the ruin of the east wall. "Screw you." He looked straight at the bearded, sunglassed man. "Screw you, especially."

"You little shit punk . . ."

Aaron probably would have made it, probably would have gotten out of Jason's reach in time, if he hadn't been standing on a jagged, crumbling pile. As it was, Jason got a hold of Aaron's T-shirt, enough to get his other arm around his chest, and he struggled to keep a hold and keep them both upright.

"Aaron, man, stand down. Stand down!

"Come on, buddy, let's take a walk. Let's take a walk, man, come on."

Jason pushed him toward the bottom of the pile, and they had to jump a gap between it and the foundation. They walked around and behind the intact west wall, away from the men and most of the watching crowd, and up to the street. The college kids pretended to work so they could watch without staring. In pockets of them here and there, within the knots in which they'd gathered, one guy among them would say something he thought was funny, and other kids would spurt laughter, and stifle more. Once Aaron walked beyond the yard they returned to their appointed tasks: mostly carrying, toting limbs and Jason's logs to one pile at the street, toting house wares and house pieces to another pile that completed their transformation into trash. Some of the students worked with donated rakes, gathering the nails and paper and tiny scraps out of the torn and weedy grass. They did what they could do, and they didn't have to be doing it.

If Jason hadn't left his chainsaw down by the poplar, he'd have put Aaron in his truck and just left. Instead he got Aaron started walking, up the ridge, toward the cross street and the next block. "Yeah, I'm good," he got Aaron to say, and when he had, he started back. He didn't know if he was walking back to get to work again, or to collect their tools and go. That depended on the others. Jason expected that, one way or another, he was walking back to calm and to explain. He expected that he could; he'd seen and heard sergeants and fire captains do it. He figured the Professor would understand, or pretend to, but he'd probably ask them to leave either way. Jason could see the situation from the Professor's position, responsible as he was for all those cared-for kids (kids, Jason thought, goddamn; we'd have gone to high school together) and their well-being. Those two men from next door might understand; they looked the right age to have served in Vietnam. Or they could have dodged it, and already Jason had learned that those were the least likely to give two shits. The two men seemed severe and hard-working, prosperous enough in whatever fields they'd chosen, and life had justified them at least to themselves. They were, in fact, just the kind of men that Jason and Aaron expected to be. That's why they'd joined up; that's why they were here now—so they could deserve some justification on down the line.

Aaron kept walking, and knew that walking was supposed to drain the temper from him, but he was just getting angrier. He could feel it whirring around inside him, spinning faster and faster and growing, straining against the confines of his skin. He could feel it crowding out all thoughts except of shame and injustice. He walked those residential streets, emptied of all the residents, between rows of volunteers' cars, stuck up and marked with team colors and yellow ribbons and the red, white and blue, and what the hell did they know, all of them assembled here to help and to be seen helping, and what could they do, what could they really do?

They'd shamed him. They'd talked to him like a damn child, like one of those college kids who didn't know or care what kind of shoes to wear into destruction. No, worse; they didn't talk to rich-ass college kids like that. What did they know about him, about who he was and what he'd done and what he deserved? All he'd been trying to do was something useful, something good.

He came upon a corner lot and noticed that no crew worked in it. The debris lay ungathered in the yard. The damage was near complete; the house had failed against the elements. Aaron heard a scurrying, a shifting from within the bricks. A man was in the pile, as Aaron had been, rummaging, searching, but without gloves, method, or heed.

Aaron watched for a minute before he said, "Buddy, you need some help?"

"You believe this shit? You believe this shit?" The man was frantic, digging at the bricks and boards with his bare hands. "I don't believe it. I don't. Jesus God."

The man stopped, stood. He shook his head. He laughed. "I wasn't feeling good. I didn't feel good, so I came home early. I came home early, and I went to sleep. I kicked off my shoes and stretched out and went to sleep. I woke up, and it was like . . . it was . . ." He shook his head again, laughed again. "It wasn't just the house shaking. It was the Earth. It was the Earth that was being shook. My poor old house just happened to be on it." He bent again to the pile.

"It's a genuine miracle. A miracle. I know. But now . . ."

Aaron had not the slightest idea of the right thing to say. The man flipped over a board, examined whatever was underneath, and put his hands to his head. "It's no use. It's no goddamn use. I can't find it."

"What are you looking for, sir?"

The man pointed across the pile. A single brown leather boot sat on a stack of bricks. "My other boot. How the hell can I get started on this without my boots?" The man clamored, stumbled, out of the pile. He sat on the grass with his legs splayed out before him and began to cry and cuss.

Aaron breathed as if he'd been struck. He climbed into the remains of the house and began to shift each constituent part.

THE OTHER SHOE

by Jennifer Horne

My dog Lucy started bringing home shoes just after we moved to a place outside of town, beyond the university perimeter zone.

At first I'd save them, hoping their partners would show up, but when they didn't I would throw them away, though it seemed a shame.

Another place we'd lived, Lucy had brought me a pair of size-7 cowboy boots, the left and then the right, a day apart. At first I worried maybe they'd come off a corpse or something, but they were clean and nearly new so I decided they'd fallen off a truck somewhere and I gave them to my sister for her birthday because she wears size-7 shoes and has learned not to ask too many questions about the provenance of her gifts from me. My all-purpose answer, which is also mostly true, is "The thrift store," or, for my more upscale friends, "A great little consignment shop."

I was out walking Lucy one day (she runs free, so the walk is mostly for me, and for companionship) when an old brown Ford pickup slowed to speak. I wasn't afraid. Beyond the u.p.z., people do that. At the very least they wave, nod, or tip-raise a finger up from the steering wheel.

This truck was driven by a redheaded, bearded, big ole guy in a T-shirt of indeterminate color.

"That your dog?"

Affirmative.

"She's been over at my place."

I hoped she hadn't caused any trouble.

"Naw, she's fine." Pause. "You new out here?"

Affirmative again. I told him we lived down past the creek—a friendly response, but not too specific, just in case he did turn out to be an ax-murderer. If he wasn't, he'd respect my being careful until I knew him better.

"You at the university?"

Guilty as charged.

"You a professor?"

No, just a librarian.

"Oh, I like books. Civil War, mostly. Some sci-fi." He said this defiantly, as though I would correct his choices.

I told him my husband read sci-fi, too. It was an easy way to sneak in the having a husband part.

I said I'd better get Lucy on home, and he said, "She ever show up with a shoe?"

Ah.

"I'm so sorry," I said. "I had no idea where they were coming from."

He smiled, which was somewhat like seeing a bear brushing its teeth—charming, but unexpected. "It don't matter. I ain't got but one foot so she can have all the left-footed shoes she wants. I just throw 'em in a pile in the yard."

He motioned for me to look inside the truck and inspect his left-footlessness, but I demurred.

"Didn't you notice they was all left-footed shoes?"

I had not.

When I got home I told Bill the whole thing. Devoted as he has become to remaining slightly drunk from noon until midnight—he jokes that if he ever started going to meetings he wouldn't need AA, just A, since he only drinks half the day—it took him a minute to grasp the various linkages of the story, but when he did he hooted, "That old redneck is just pulling your leg—so to speak!"

I defended the one-footedness of the pickup truck guy, but Bill was adamant. After supper I secretly turned down the air conditioner beyond

16

where he likes it and went out on the porch to listen to the cicadas. Lucy followed. Loyal dog.

Time passed. Leaves fell. The occasional left-footed shoe turned up in the yard. Lucy chewed them until the novelty wore off, then I put them in the trash. Truck guy and I would wave sometimes when I was out walking.

One full-moon night I was wakeful until midnight but then fell into a deep and dreaming sleep, so strong in its reality I thought I was still awake. I walked out into my backyard, which was also my childhood backyard, and there was my dead mother sitting in a lawn chair. Her hair was long and flowing, the way it was at night after she'd let it down and brushed it out, and she was wearing a ruby colored, full length zip-up robe. She looked like royalty. I was so happy to see her, and she rose and hugged me. She was smiling as though she'd just discovered a gold ring in a flower bed, and she was holding a shoe.

"Do you know what this is?" she asked. "It's the other shoe. All my life I've been waiting for the other shoe to drop, and now it has, and there's nothing to be afraid of anymore. Isn't it wonderful?"

I felt my heart glow in my chest like a picture I'd once seen of the Blessed Virgin Mary, and we both stood there laughing and looking into each other's eyes.

Just before Thanksgiving, on my way home from work, late because we'd had an event at the library I had to do the A/V for, I stopped to get milk in the little country store on the corner before you go down the road that leads to our road. Bill has ulcers and at least will always drink milk, even if he is otherwise not attentive to his health.

I rarely go there. The prices are higher and the selection minimal. Some of the cans are now in the vintage category. But I did not want to go to the regular store at that hour just for milk. Something about a grocery store at dusk makes me weepy.

The door opened with its cheerful ding, and as I headed down the aisle, saltine crackers on one side of me and potted meats on the other, I saw in front of me my redheaded Ford friend, both feet planted firmly on the poured concrete floor.

He glanced up from the restaurant-size can of pork and beans he was holding like it was a football, looked back down at the can, then back at me.

"Hey, it's the dog lady! I mean—"

"Yeah, it's okay," I said. "I know what you meant. How you doing?"

"Can't complain. Getting dark earlier, isn't it?"

"Yep. We walk mostly early mornings these days."

"Hmm."

"Lucy brought home another shoe yesterday," I said.

His face changed. He looked sad beyond belief. "Oh." He looked down at his feet, very obviously a pair. "I am so sorry. I really am. I didn't mean to tell you no lie."

I had to know. "Well, where do the shoes come from?"

He smiled with the wiliness of a country boy, sensing himself already semi-forgiven. "Well, I work for my cousin sometimes, doing construction. Deconstruction, really—but not like that Derrida, nothing philosophical. Just simple deconstruction—I help take the buildings down."

I waited. I was not going to be distracted by a tossed-off allusion to Derrida.

"And you'd be surprised how many old leather shoes you find at these places, sometimes in a closet, sometimes under the porch. I throw 'em in the truck, take 'em home and compost 'em."

But why, I asked, would he only find left shoes?

He looked sad again. "Well, they're both. I just thought you probably wouldn't have noticed. Then after I told you that tale I had to start taking out the right-footed ones."

Tired, a little irritable from work, I felt exasperated with myself for having fallen for his joke, angry at Bill for his cynicism in being right. I sighed and turned to go.

"Hey. I'm sorry I told you a story. You just looked like someone who would *like* there to be a good story about all them shoes."

What could I say? He was right. I would rather have a made-up good story than the actual boring truth, and that is why I still thought Bill was a misunderstood genius artist and that someday all Republicans would see the light.

The checkout girl seemed to be containing a smile as she rang up my milk. I went out into the cooling dark and headed home.

I had kept the last shoe that showed up, a brown leather boot, because it had writing on it, in black ink, like a rune. I thought it might help me figure something out. I don't know what. It was just that it was like a clue.

The boot was still sitting on top of the doghouse, where I had put it out of Lucy's reach, when I got home. Looking at it more closely now, I could see that the letters and hearts and stars had probably been drawn by some lovesick teenage girl, not a mysterious one-footed redneck. All the same, I tucked the boot under my arm and took it out to the porch with me after I'd put Bill's milk in the fridge.

Lucy joined me, sniffed briefly at the boot, then tucked her nose under my thigh and nuzzled me as I studied the markings. I was determined to make some sense of it after all, even if it was not the story I'd thought it was going to be.

A SIN OF OMISSION

by Jim Wilson

I never told anybody, not until now, but it was my fault my dad shot our bird dog. It was an accident, but it was still my fault. I didn't realize at the time I was to blame, that my sin of omission had brought Jo close to death one warm December afternoon at the edge of a cornfield in Granville County while I was off at college in Chapel Hill.

From the first moment I remember watching my dad reach into the game bag of his hunting coat and remove, one by one, half a dozen plump little bobwhites, I knew I would be a quail man. The realization was sudden and visceral, striking like true love or 190-proof liquor. This would be who I was. My dad handed me each bird, and I stroked their feathers. Each made good weight in my hand. He smiled when I pulled a bird to my nose and smelled it, inhaled that aroma of winter woods and earth and broom straw and decay, a fragrant essence hinting of wildness and cold and secluded dark places. What dog wouldn't relish putting his nose down into that gravy?

Later, I walked in my dad's steps to the back of our yard where the grass gave out and dark woods began and watched as he gutted and plucked the birds. His fingers, sticky with blood and clotted with feathers, moved quickly over each one. My dad explained that the birds with the white throat patch and eye stripes were males, and that the females had buff-colored patches and stripes. When he removed their entrails, he held up heart, liver, gizzard and intestines like some pagan priest and named them before tossing them into the woods. He opened the crop of each bird and showed me the seeds inside: milo, soybeans, beggar lice and some unidentifiable weeds. Their crops were full; they had eaten well that day. We would eat well the next day.

From such beginnings—a rustic tableau once common between fathers and sons in the South—was born a lifelong obsession for bob-white quail. It is a love that surpasses my comprehension. I don't try to understand it any longer; I simply accept that thoughts and images of quail hunting evoke something instinctive for me, something neither rational nor irrational. I suspect I am not alone in this sentiment, for I have come to recognize the wistful stares in other men when they see a golden broom straw field or a red clay field or hear the distant call of cock bobwhite.

Love and Death

I love those birds, yet I kill them and eat them. How can you kill a thing you love? It is a mystery as old as human hunting, an ancient primal question. Of prehistoric hunters anthropologist Wade Davis says, "Every day, you had to kill the thing you loved most, the animals upon which your life was dependent. It was the first mystery—and I would argue the basis of religion, which was an attempt to explain what happens after you die."

As an initiate, I revered the trappings of the bobwhite brother-hood—the tan Duxbak canvas coat with the hidden pocket inside for cigarettes, the brush pants and the tall leather boots that required frequent oiling to attain a small measure of water resistance. While it was the coat I loved first, I realized years later that the boots were more valuable to a man who walks all day, as bird hunters do. It wouldn't be the last time I'd love the wrong thing first. I did grow tired of my dad's constant admonitions to clean the mud off my boots, to keep them in a warm place so they might dry. Eventually we came to have cleaning sessions, sharing a can of mink oil at the kitchen table as we worked the paste into every crevice of our boots.

"You can tell a lot about a man by his boots," my dad would say as we massaged the leather. "Dirty boots are a sign of carelessness and laziness."

The lessons took, and over the years the routine of cleaning boots, even when they don't need it, has become a brief haven. And I guess I grew good at it, too. The last night I spent in the same house with my ex-wife she asked if I would polish her Danskos before I left. I did. They looked good.

If you love quail, then you must love bird dogs. Pointers, setters and spaniels are the *sine qua non*—the "without which not"—of quail hunting. You can quail hunt without a dog, but it is a miserable, unsatisfying shade of a thing that's not worth the effort. It's like kissing a picture of your girlfriend instead of her lips.

My dad had brought Jo home a couple of years before I began quail hunting. She was a tiny, delicate-looking black-and-white pointer-setter mix who, knowing my dad's frugal nature, was probably the runt of the litter, the dog least likely to succeed, the pup nobody wanted. I was happy to have her. My dad let me name her, and I chose Josie because of my fascination with a character in a book I was reading. (Actually, I was enamored of this fictional farm girl with brown hair and dreamed of bringing home to her a coat full of bobwhites. What she might ever do with them I never considered. The gesture, the moment of relinquishing something of value to another, was what mattered.)

Against the odds, including my dad's admitted shortcomings as a bird dog trainer, Jo became the best dog I've ever hunted over. She was birdy from the beginning and loved to hunt bobwhites, probably more than I did. In the field, she was quick but thorough, working best after being given free rein to disappear for about fifteen minutes and scrub off some repressed energy. She was not a woman who would lie to you. If Jo said there were no birds in that strip of partridge peas, there were no birds in that strip of partridge peas. And if my dad or I called out, "Hunt up, Jo. Hunt up," because we thought she had been too hasty in her assessment of a birdy-looking spot, she would turn to the offender with a look of sad bemusement that seemed to say, "I'll do it, but it ain't going to make any birds come flying out of there."

By late afternoon the end of her tail would be bloody from beating against brush and briers. I reckoned it her badge of honor, just as the scratched and bleeding backs of my hands were my badge of bird-hunting authenticity.

Often I hunted alone with Jo. I like hunting with others, but going alone also is good. Sometimes it's the best way. When I was sixteen, Jo and I were hunting, walking down the railroad track, our shortcut from a cornfield to a milo field. She was fifty yards down the track, and I was walking slowly, my shotgun held over my forearm and pointing toward the ground. Suddenly, I heard a bang and gravel scattered six inches from my right foot. I responded with every cuss word I knew at the time. I've since added considerably to my vocabulary.

Frantically, I looked at my boot to make sure blood wasn't flowing, but I was alright. I figured I must have absentmindedly slipped the safety and touched the trigger for the right-hand barrel. *I can't tell anybody about this*, I thought, *because I might not be allowed to hunt*. That was the important thing, the preservation of my hunting days. And so I immediately plotted a strategy of silence. I was unhurt, and no one would know what had happened.

Out of Mind

For several weeks the incident lingered in my thoughts whenever I picked up my shotgun, an aged Charles Daly 12-gauge featherweight, a gun that, if you weren't careful mounting it, would smack you harder than your mama when you misbehaved in church. Gradually, like so much that comprises our days, the incident faded from memory, and I no longer fretted over the fact that I had nearly—literally—shot myself in the foot.

Another quail season passed, another Thanksgiving and Christmas spent pursuing bobwhites with my dad and Jo. The three of us, and sometimes a neighbor or my brother, Sam, hunted hard into the winter, through January and February until near darkness on the very last day of the season. I loved the cold hunting, the rough, frozen fields, the dying sun glinting on broom straw, and the slicing wind on my cheeks that sent snot running unchecked from my nose. Then came college, and our quail-hunting triumvirate was now but two on most days. I thought often of the birds and Jo and my dad as late autumn arrived and I struggled to accustom myself to living inside city limits for the first time in my life. I thought myself to sleep in those days by retracing our hunts, trampling from one covert to another in a piece of poor country where I longed to be. It rained without stop over most of Thanksgiving break, and the red fields turned to mire under dark, gray skies, and we did not hunt. Christmas, I thought, would be different.

In early December, my dad and Jo hunted one of our favorite fields, the big one near the lake that often had corn or wheat planted in it, the one with the low area in the middle that most times had a few inches of standing water and occasionally contained a mallard or two. My dad killed one quail with a single shot on the covey rise, and Jo retrieved the bird. As she approached within a few feet, bobwhite in mouth, my dad, the side-by-side angled across his left arm, reached to take the bird. The gun fired, hitting Jo in the top of her neck and slamming back the gun's top lever, splitting the web of flesh between my dad's thumb and index finger.

Jo lay bleeding on the ground, her legs pawing the air as though she were running. My dad took off his hunting coat, wrapped it about her and carried her to the car and on to the veterinarian's office, where Jo was medicated, stitched and cared for. She slept on a hastily fashioned bed of old blankets on the back porch throughout her recovery, which eventually was all but complete. She was the lone dog my dad ever allowed in the house. Only a small scar remained where her coat did not grow back as it should have. She showed no disinclination to hunt, no fear of shotgun blasts. She was a bird dog; that was her life, and she would not be denied her nature or her pleasure.

It was a couple of weeks after the accident, with Jo still lying on the blankets and watching me with her dark brown eyes as I'd walk past, when my dad asked if I wanted to ride along to the gunsmith shop. "I want to make sure there's nothing wrong with that side-by-side," he said. "I know the safety was on; I can't figure out why it went off like that." After hearing the story of what had happened to Jo, the gunsmith began taking apart the shotgun. He held up a piece and said, "I'm sure you've got a weak trigger spring. I'm surprised it hasn't been a problem before."

Fault and Blame

That's when I knew: It was my fault. I should have figured something was wrong with the gun. I could have prevented the whole thing if I'd only confessed to nearly shooting myself in the foot. Again I remained silent, adding that to the secret list of things that I would not talk about. I would think about it, take it out and hold it up as an example of my many failures, but I wouldn't speak of it.

Jo lived to thirteen years of age before she simply failed to wake one morning, the best way of all for a dog, or a man, to go. My dad wasn't so lucky. After surgery for a spot on one of his lungs, within nine months his doctors found that the cancer had spread to his brain. Even though he died within six weeks of his diagnosis, his was not an easy death. As the summer lengthened, my father lost the ability to speak and then to move. I could only watch as he became less and less of the man I had known, a shade of what he used to be when I was young and he schooled me in the pastimes of country boys, of hunting, fishing and baseball. As he lingered, I sat in his room and watched him slip toward death and cursed his dissolute and disinterested angels for failing to keep him safe. There was nothing I could do. I felt I should rest my hand on his or touch his gaunt, whiskered face, but I didn't. We are not a demonstrative family; we keep ourselves to ourselves. It is our way. He died alone in early morning darkness on a July day when the sun came up white and the air was dry and hot at first light.

In the days following his death, the most natural and comforting thought was of the three of us hunting. Jo holds point at the end of a brown field flanked on three sides by a catbrier and honeysuckle thicket. My dad approaches from the right, I from the left, and as we close, the covey erupts from the field stubble. We begin to mount our guns. I freeze the image while we remain in motion, as though holding that unfinished act gives them life everlasting. John Keats learned that two hundred years ago after admiring a scene on a Grecian urn. I figured it out while picturing a Southern factory worker and a cheap bird dog hunting red clay North Carolina fields. That is the image of us I keep, the one I cherish.

My dad quit quail hunting after Jo died. I never asked why, but I think I understand now. I, however, was only twenty years old and eager to find a new dog, anxious to resume the hunt. And hunt I did, although despite having a number of bird dogs, I never found one as good as Jo. Even today when I am quail hunting, I always picture Jo, her tail held high and bloody, her jowls quivering with the scent of quail on the ground.

I have a friend who says there is no always, and I myself am cautious of the word. It's an easy word, one often uttered without thought and empty of the forever it promises. But I know she is wrong. I believe in always; I always have. Always is a rare thing. You don't often have it within your grasp. You do, however, know it when you find it, and you'd best hold hard to it. Jo was an always kind of dog.

Decades after I failed to tell my dad of my accident, I still sometimes think of my negligence, usually on nights when I'm feeling I haven't measured up in some way to some self-imposed standard, when the ghosts of regret hover by my side and hiss aloud my failures in the darkness. I could have prevented harm to a man and a dog—my dad, my dog. I let them down, and they never knew. I'd like to apologize now, but there's no one left who would give a damn.

 FLIGHT

by Shari Smith

I took the barstool at the corner, well away from the small gathering of men at the other end.

I came to listen to the woman and her guitar. I ordered a beer and pulled the phone from my pocket to send the word, wanting him to know where I was.

Just in case.

She sang a song I knew better than she did, about a Captured Angel, waiting to make a break. I've known that song since an old friend brought the vinyl album named for it to my house in a place I would fly away from as soon as I could kick the cage door open and I have been living the lyrics ever since.

I've done some damage. I've hurt men who did not deserve it because they failed to see the tattered edges and missing feathers in my wings, wings that drag the ground, collecting the dust of a road I hear call me all too often, a call I tend to answer, sooner or later. They either believed they could quiet the call or it did go silent long enough for me to believe it, too, that this one would stick. I would make a list of all the reasons I should stay when wind howled through pines and whispered to a gypsy soul I have come to accept, as those frayed wings began to gather around me, keeping pleas of love or logic from ever reaching any place that could feel it.

It wasn't always my fault. A few of the scars in the soft downy layer, the lining designed to keep out bitter cold and drowning rain, were not of my making. I found rocks to throw myself against either in blindness to their ability to wound me or the belief that I deserved it. But, leaving is what I know. No shackles yet have kept me from it once I've made up my mind to take flight. It has saved me, more than once.

It's been a while, now, that I've thought, maybe, this was the one. I keep waiting to hear the highway, to feel the feathers pick up a breeze. It doesn't come.

I paid for my beer telling the bartender I would only be having one. No need to run a tab. He came, waving another bottle at me anyway, said a gentleman wanted to buy it for me, wondered would I take it. Five stools down, there was a nod when I thanked him. He moved in, three closer. He asked if I was from around there and laughed when I said, "Claremont," not knowing that's about as quick a way to piss me off as any there is. He asked me what I did for a living before he ran out of questions and said he liked Tom Clancy but just the movies, not the books. I started to feel sorry for him when he told me he didn't like this bar, this town, or sports because "they're mindless." I told him, in fact, they were not.

I checked my phone, again.

A few more questions occurred to him. He asked if I knew a really old song called "Pretty Woman" and I laughed, though I did try not to. He said I was pretty and I thanked him for that. He asked if my writing was "like, a thing?" and I said it was exactly like a thing. He shook his head and said he worked in a factory that made furniture. He hated that, too. He asked me if I knew Thomas Hunter. It took him describing a movie before I realized he was referring to Hunter S. Thompson and told him that, no, I did not know him and even if I did, he was dead by his own hand and I was beginning to understand why. He didn't get that joke.

I checked my phone and smiled, thinking of a man who would.

He asked me why I had on cowboy boots, if I liked "horses or something." I told him I always wear them. He said they looked like they'd hurt and used the bar for balance to show me his Adidas knockoffs, said he preferred comfort to having his toes squished together in the pointed end of a boot but he reckoned I'd have a hard time running away in those boots so I'd be easier to catch. His comfortable shoes did not spare him the pinch when I said I didn't need fast shoes to know how to get gone.

He spoke of his brother which was a chance I didn't let pass. "How old is he?" I asked him. He said he was his age, thirty-one, then corrected himself and said he was close to his age. I sent a text, couldn't help it. The bartender gave me a look and raised his chin, a silent offer to intervene, but I shook it off. He didn't know. He couldn't see those wings from where he was standing.

Before he would give up he would ask if I wanted to friend him on Facebook and confess that he had lied about his age, that he was, in truth, twenty-nine, but he guessed I might be in my thirties so he thought he should be, too. There might have been a time when that flattered me. I reckon most women would have been but I wasn't blessed with that kind of mind.

I checked my phone, again, sent a message and reached for my coat.

I learned a long time ago what I don't want. I'm learning what it is I do. I still believe that there is a higher love and I am capable of it, of having it, of earning it. I like taking care of a man. I like the work of it. I tried, for a time, to not like it but with enough road passing under you, you learn to accept things about yourself even as your children or your best friends beg you to change them. I like to cook and watch a man enjoying eating. I like to fold shirts the way he wants to find them in his drawer. I will press a crease in jeans if that is the way he wears them. I will give him a thousand smiles and it will cost him nothing.

And, I will wait for him to notice that there is no crying baby I cannot rock to sleep, no song I have heard more than twice without being able to recite the lyrics. I will wait for him to read the words I write and find the reason I chose them. I will wait for him to believe that music and magic live in me, that I can see things others miss because of the best thing about me which is that I pay attention.

But I won't wait forever.

I will fly. It's what I know. I cannot be captured even though it is often what I wish for. A smart and sexy man once said to me that I was waiting for someone to tell me it's all going to be alright. I told him that it wasn't hard to get someone to tell me that. It was impossible for me to believe it.

If my wings are smaller these days, they are stronger. I find that I use them less and less for flight but still, sometimes, for cover. I think less like a captured angel and more like a fallen one, still believing that there is coming a moment when I can say, and mean, take anything you want from me, anything...

And I will hear it said back to me.

And the highway will be dark and the winds will be still and the only sound will be breathing with no separation in rhythm or depth and the wings, though there, will be remembered for having brought me to that place where I know it's alright.

It's alright.

ALL THE WAY TO MEMPHIS

by Suzanne Hudson

Clista Juniper was a meticulous woman, from her immaculate house-keeping to her perfectly enunciated sentences to the way she presided over the Tender County High School Library in southern Mississippi. It even extended to her daily wardrobe, which consisted of tailored suits in every shade of beige so that the coral lips and nails, with matching pumps, her trademark, would stand out all the more, her platinum-dyed hair double-French-twisted in a tight, inwardly curling, labial sheen, à la Tippi Hedren. Indeed, her colleagues—for she had no real intimates—often teased her about her early sixties look, whereupon Clista might express her practiced, breathy giggle and respond, "It is me, the look. Always has been."

"Right down to the girdle?" a teacher might ask.

"Absolutely."

"With the clips and all?" another might chime in.

"Certainly."

"They still make those?"

"I have always believed in stocking up."

"What's a girdle?" a neophyte, a young woman poorly read who took no note of puns, might ask.

So Clista, though she was senior staff at sixty-something, would leave it to another woman, a fifty-something, to explain, getting back to her shelves and her silence and her computerized Dewey decimal system (although she maintained a card catalogue as well), shushing students with a coral pucker against her coral-nailed index finger.

The automobile she was driving on this day, her champagne-colored Cadillac, was as meticulously kept as she, although, on this particular day, she was thinking of taking up a former bad habit and filling the car's ashtray with coral-printed filters on the butts of fags she had smoked. She was on edge, shaky, the twists of her coif slightly wispy, like the frayed nerves she so tightly held inside the emotions she rarely let loose. She had let loose this morning, though, before doing her usual ablutions and her makeup, stepping into her heels and into the Cadillac and driving not to the high school, where she would be expected after the weekend, but north, to some indeterminate place, she knew not where.

When she saw the figure in the distance, on the side of the highway, she knew immediately what she would do. Clista was nothing like the sort to pick up a hitchhiker, but she would certainly make an exception on this day, as she put her life, her profession, her town behind her, making a sure-to-be futile attempt to run away. This was a day of making all kinds of breaks, a day for the shattering of facades, the clattering of realities, a day to step out of character and try to locate her self, if there ever was such a thing. It made a crazy kind of ironic sense to pick up a hitcher, who, as she drew closer, looked more and more like a teenage girl, finally becoming one, sturdy but slight of frame, like a gymnast. Certainly not threatening, like the haggard and tattooed serial-killer stereotype that had forever lived in Clista's wagons-circled mind. She pulled to the shoulder of the road and watched in the rearview mirror as the girl gathered up her things and bounded toward the waiting vehicle. Catching her own eyes in the reflecting oval of silvered glass, she saw a shadow of the emotion and primal fear that had captured her in the pre-dawn hours this morning, when she shot and killed her husband of forty-something years.

It was only an oddity to her now that she had done such a thing; it seemed distant and sketchily surreal. Strange how rapidly those tautly bound emotions came undone, ramping into the kind of sight-blotted rage that would allow a person to do murder, settling afterwards into a numbness of spirit and mind that allowed her to believe in the possibility of simply running away—almost to believe it had never happened in the first place. The numbness vibrated in an ear-humming buzz, as if her entire skull were swaddled in layer upon layer of cotton sheeting or felt, but there were fuzzy sounds of car doors and heavy canvas bags thudding into the leather seats. Then a voice, a face, something like words.

"What?" Clista managed.

"It's just that you've saved my life, that's all. If I had to be in this nothing place just one more day, just one more day, I would go nut case. See, my family is an insane asylum. My dope fiend mother especially. And so I just now packed up my shit, marched my butt down that dirt lane, and sat myself on the side of the highway. And here you come right off the bat. Shit, what's your name?"

It was a jarring question, and inside of Clista's hesitation, her guest continued.

"I'm Savannah. But I don't think I'll keep that name. It's just not the blues. Savannah. It's a city in Georgia, not a bluesy person. Oh, what about Georgia? For a name, I mean. Do you have any chips or something? I'm always hungry. I'm definitely set on a different speed than most other people. Are you going to put it in drive?"

Again the out-of-left-field questions caught Clista off guard. "I— yes," she said, pulling back onto the pavement. Ever prepared for emergencies, she gestured at the glove box, where Savannah found a pack of cheese crackers.

The girl tore into the package with her teeth, orange crumbs scattering, then, "I love states for names—Bama, Carolina. Cities, not so much. Missouri is nice. What's yours?"

"My—"

"Name."

"It's Clista," she said, thinking, *and I murdered my husband this morning, because he did the unimaginable and betrayed our decades of sameness and safety and "understoods," and "inasmuchases" and such immaculate respectability as most couples never achieve. He took all that was invested in our public presentation as a couple and crumbled every iota of trust into talcum powder and the fairy dust that magically transformed me into a cold, cold killer.*

"—so of course you know that," Savannah was saying.

"Know what?"

"What I was saying. Are you alright? I was saying how your name sounds something like a female part, but I guess you caught a lot of teasing at a certain age, so of course you know that. Junior high is hell for everybody." She sucked in a breath. "I'm sorry if I offended you. Sometimes I go over the top. My mind goes faster than I can talk and I try to keep up and so words get blurted out before I know it. You know?"

Clista was not accustomed to such talk, talk of female parts with sexual references, cursing, and just plain chattiness of a distasteful bent, as she had no good best girlfriend, having kept the world at a polite, respectable distance. This girl, however, felt unthreatening in spite of her verbiage. "How old are you?" Clista attempted, to divert.

"Twenty-six," was the reply. "I know, I know. I look sixteen. I get it all the time. It's because I'm so small-boned. And flat-chested. I've thought about store-bought tits, implants, but I just don't believe in doing that shit to your body." She sighed with a flourish. "It's a blessing and a curse, being my size. I mean, when I tell people I'm a blues singer, they laugh. 'Ain't no big, bluesy voice gonna come out of that little thing.' Plus I'm white, obviously. 'Little bitty white chicks can't sing the blues.' Folks just don't take me seriously. When you've lived through the low down dirty shit I've lived through, you can damn sure feel the hurt. Like, what do you do when it takes your crackhead mother two years to get rid of a man who's messing with you and you're nine years old? Two years!"

"Oh, my!" Clista drew away from her, on instinct, and was immediately embarrassed.

"Well, it wasn't my fault, you know."

"Of course not. Absolutely not. I'm so sorry. I'm just not accustomed—"

"My point is that's just one of the crappy things I've experienced. And it wasn't even the worst. But I keep it upbeat, you know? Keep it in the sunlight. Positive thoughts. Let it out in the lyrics. So do you believe I can sing?"

"I would imagine so," thinking, *betrayal feels like the big, silver blade of a very sharp knife slicing cleanly through the jugular. He betrayed me and I was unleashed in an unthinkable way, into utter insanity. I was not responsible, nor do I regret. The lioness kills to protect her vulnerable offspring, after all. Is there an analo-*

gy to be had? Does it even matter?

"—and my boyfriend—he's a tattoo artist—he did all of mine, see?" She turned her leg to reveal the serpent-like lizard inked around her calf, winding toward its own tail, turned a shoulder bearing a crucifix, Jesus and his blood upon an elaborately detailed cross, the eyes of the Holy Martyr cast up in surrender to the Father. "His name—my boyfriend's—is Dakota. A state, right? It fits with my worldview. He is amazingly talented. I mean, isn't this gorgeous?" She pulled down the front of her T-shirt to reveal, just above her heart, a small but beautifully intricate insect of some kind—something like one might find in a fly-fisherman's tackle box. "I have others, but they are in hard-to-find places, if you know what I mean."

Clista's husband was a fly-fisherman with a vast, three-tiered tackle box loaded with treasured lures, some even from his navy days, the days of their courtship. He took regular and frequent fishing trips to Colorado at solitary resorts, to the Rocky Mountain streams where he danced his line in the rhythmic ballet of a cast. She did not accompany him, as she had no interest in his hobbies other than as fodder for those sometimes necessary social conversations:

"Paul loves his lures as much as he loves me," she might joke, "but at least he finds me more alluring." Not that she alluded to any sort of physical sensuality between the two of them. Clista had always found that particular expression of human instinct to be distasteful at best, more of the time disgusting. There were unartful fumblings early in their union, a marriage that followed a courteous courtship, but they soon settled into a life of platonic rhythms, ebbing away into their separate lives of a day and then flowing into their dining room and den of an evening, watching the woods at night from their isolated split-level home, tucking into the twin beds connected by a nightstand bearing an antique Princess telephone, pink, with a nine-millimeter loaded and at the ready in its French Provincial drawer.

"—so why don't you just take a look." Savannah had opened a cell phone and was scrolling through some photographs. "Here you go." She turned the screen to Clista.

"Oh!" It came almost as a shriek paired with another recoiling of her whole body. The wheels left the blacktop for a few seconds.

"Holy Christ—what was that?" Savannah looked at her as if she had two heads and then studied the screen of her phone, a close-up of her pubic area and the peace lily engraved above the curls. Her face fell. "Oh. I thought you wanted to see my other tattoos. Sorry."

"No, it's alright. I—I'm just not accustomed to such images."

"No shit. Well, I didn't mean to scare you. I mean, it's just skin, basically. I've never seen what the big deal is. Skin is skin. It holds in our organs. Sex is something else, but it really amounts to just rubbing. But you're the driver so I sure as hell won't fuck with you. But you have to know up front that I was born without a filter."

"Filter?"

"You know, I tend to blurt out whatever's in my head. I'm ADHD, so it kind of goes with the territory. I'll try to watch my mouth, though. I mean, you could easily just dump me on the side of the road again. And there I'd be with my thumb out. Again."

"I won't do that." Then, for no real reason she could fathom, Clista added, "I'm going all the way to Memphis."

"For real? Holy shit, that's awesome. How lucky is it you picked me up? And don't worry—no more tattoo pictures," and she laughed a trilling, lively laugh.

Paul had a tattoo, from the time he served in the navy during the Vietnam conflict. It was of two intertwining snakes encircling a cross, the word *Bound* crowning the cross like a bent halo. He said it represented his love of country, how bound up in it he was. And he believed in what he was doing, fighting the Red Menace off the shores of Southeast Asia, even if he never had to dodge any bullets.

"Your husband?"

"What?" Clista had not realized she had spoken.

"With the serpents. So symbolic. I mean, my Uncle Jessie actually fought over there—lost a leg and an eye. He has a cool glass eye he always entertained us with—my cousins and me—when we were kids. He'd take it out and toss it up in the air and catch it in his mouth like popcorn."

Clista shuddered.

"I know, pretty gross. But not if you're a little kid and not really at all if you think. I mean, look what he's been through. He deserves to do whatever the hell he wants, huh? He doesn't have a fake leg anymore. He used to. And he could make it do fart noises, another thing little kids love."

"Goodness!" Paul was not allowed—had not been allowed—to fart in her presence. Clista insisted that he step into the bathroom or outside if that urge was upon him. On those occasions when it happened serendipitously, he apologized with abject humiliation to her stony disdain.

Black earth was turned in the fields bordering Highway 61. It was planting time and within months the black dirt would turn to snow, and cotton puffs would litter the roadside after picking was done. Picking. To pick off. She had killed him, shot him in the head right there in his study, where she had found him before dawn, crept up to the door, borne witness to the sounds of lecherous, staccato-rhythmed motions and gritty, profane talk. He was preoccupied enough not to notice the slight click as she eased the door open, just a crack, just enough so that she could see the man facing him on the computer screen. She knew immediately who he was—the man in the photographs holding stringers heavy-laden with fish, the best friend from the navy, Spencer Kraus, also married. She fetched the gun and returned to wait it out. He did not notice, even when the screen had gone dark and he had laid his head down onto his arms, exhausted, as she padded across pile in one dreamlike motion, squeezed two bullets into his skull, turned and left just that quickly, with the stealth of a jungle cat.

"So tell me more." Savannah's words, again jarring.

"What do you mean?"

"You just said you were a cat."

"What?"

"Yeah, a jungle cat. And I'm thinking, what the hell?"

"I'm sorry," Clista stammered. "I'm just upset." She had to watch her words, slipping out unintended and quick, like minnows darting across currents.

"Well, then tell it, sister. What did the son of a bitch do?" She pulled out a pack of American Spirit cigarettes. "Okay if I smoke?"

"Yes." Her surrender felt like the beginning of some kind of relief. "But only if you light one for me."

The sound of clattering dishes and running water came from the kitchen in the back of the diner. Savannah was putting heart and soul into devouring her sandwich, dousing it mid-chew and frequently with Dr. Pepper. "Thank you so much for buying," she gulped. "My money situation is pretty busy, but that'll change when I hook up with Dakota."

Clista had attempted to force down a salad, but nausea made that impossible so she nibbled a couple of Saltines. She had bought her very own pack of cigarettes, Virginia Slim menthols, the brand of her younger years. *You've come a long way, baby,* the old advertising jingle rattled around in her head. She exhaled a mushroom cloud of smoke. "I can't think, can't know what to do."

"Sure you can." Savannah leaned across the table, speaking in a hushed but animated tone. "You can absolutely know what to do. You just have to connect all the dots. That's what My Uncle Jessie used to say, anyway. But he was pretty PTSD. You're probably kind of PTSD about now, too."

"The dots are scattered, all across the floor," and she thought of throwing jacks as a child, the scattering stars, the ball bouncing. "That's the way the ball bounces," she murmured, smiling.

"Okay, okay, you're not going all mental on me, right?"

"No. I've already been mental. Can I go sane on you?"

"That would be good, but dude, your life is going to go end over end either way. I mean, you've got to either get a new identity and disappear—and that's really hard—or go back and come clean—and that's really hard, too. Man!" Her eyes widened at the enormousness of it all.

"Are my eyes still red and puffy?"

"Yeah, but that's good. I think it keeps the waitress from coming over too often."

Clista took out her compact and applied a fresh coat of coral to her lips. *I am a coral snake.* She blotted with a napkin pulled from the stainless-steel holder.

They were in a desolate part of the state, where the crook of the Mississippi separated Arkansas, Tennessee and Mississippi, at Buck's Diner, where time had stopped decades earlier, an eatery with worn red plastic seats, dull chrome, and a hanging musk of aged bacon grease. It was just past the lunch hour, so the two women had the place to themselves while a sour-faced teenager bused a few tables. A grizzled-looking cook sat at a booth near the kitchen door, smoking, chatting in a low, gravelly voice with the one waitress, who sauntered over to the travelers once in a while, called them "honey" and "sugar" and "baby" as she offered more tea.

"Man, you're in some serious shit. I've known all kinds of people slogging through all kinds of shit. Hell, my own mother only had me because she couldn't afford another abortion. She was a drug addict. Cocaine. Sometimes she did men to get money for it. Now she's killing herself with meth. I was trying to help her get straight, but that stuff is insane. In-fucking-sane. You really saved my life by picking me up."

A hopeful little ripple went through Clista. "Do you think maybe that cancels out the other?"

"Maybe so," Savannah grinned. "Maybe the karma is right now. Maybe that's a reason to keep running. Or to go back."

"I can't believe I actually told you everything. It's not like me at all."

"But it is me. Seriously. It's something about me," Savannah said. "People tell me stuff all the time. Strangers. I mean, I'll be in the check-out line and somebody will just unload their whole entire bizarre life story. It happens all the freaking time."

But I don't confide in anyone, Clista thought, still marveling at how Savannah had coaxed the darkness out of her.

"What did the son of a bitch do?" she had asked.

"How do you know it's about a man?"

"Always is. Your husband?"

"Yes."

"So come on with it."

"No."

"Come on. Tell it."

"I can't."

"Just say the words."

And Clista's fingers had tightened on the steering wheel of the smoke-filled, champagne-colored Cadillac. "My husband betrayed me."

"You know it."

"He lied and cheated and did it from the start."

"Uh-huh."

41

"And it's worse than that."

"How?"

"My husband betrayed me."

"Tell."

"With a man."

"Holy Christ."

"A double life."

"You're right. That is worse. Way fucking worse."

"I was faithful to that man forever and he was faithful to his man forever and I caught him in a despicable act and I killed him."

"Killed?"

"Shot."

"The fuck you say!" And Savannah had turned to fully face her in the car. "You are so not the type!"

"Apparently I am." And she had pulled onto the shoulder of the road, rested her head on the steering wheel and howled like a wounded animal as Savannah, effervescence disarmed by the rawness of it all, tried impotently to console her.

The waitress sauntered over. "Here, sweetie, let me get this out of your way." She began collecting plates and utensils, blood-red fingernails clicking against heavy white glass.

Savannah picked up the last of her BLT and pushed the plate. "Are you still taking me to Memphis?" she asked as the waitress sauntered away.

"Of course."

"You're not, like, dangerous or anything, right?" It was almost a whisper.

"I have no weapons or designs upon your possessions."

"I know that. It just felt like a question I had to ask, you know? I mean, how dumb would I feel if something really happened—and I know it isn't—but something happened and I never even asked the question in the first place. Man, would I feel dumb."

"Certainly."

"Plus, I just got to get to Memphis."

"What will you do when you get to there? Where will you live?"

"With Dakota, of course. He'll come pick me up wherever you and I land. He has a place off Beale Street, right in the thick of things. Man, I can't wait to go out to some of those clubs. Not the touristy ones on the main drag. The real ones. The ones you have to just happen into. But the first thing I'm going to do—and I know this is stupid and touristy and all—but I'm going to get me some barbecue."

"Can I join you?"

"Sure. Are you like, buying?"

"Of course. It'll be my last supper."

"Holy shit. You're not going all suicidal or anything, are you? Because that's even more messed up than what's gone down. Seriously."

"You're right. Besides, I don't know. Could I actually go home to that—mess, and put the gun to my own head? I just don't see it."

"Well, you know they say it's a permanent solution to a temporary problem, right?"

"It would certainly be a problem for both my permanent and my temple," Clista said, but her puny, half-hearted attempt at punning fell on deaf ears.

Memphis was a presence she could feel well before hitting the outskirts. It was in the whispery thrum of potential stories in song—a spiritual imprint that webbed out and out to the rising hills and farms, cascading down the Mississippi River to rich Delta dirt.

Savannah must have felt it, too. She threw her head back and let fly a couple of bars of melodic anguish, big and rich, at odds with the tiny vessel making the music. "You might think you're living large, baby, but you'll be dying when you get home. You might think you're hitting the mark, baby, but you'll just be trying when you get home." She turned to Clista. "What do you think? It's something I've been working on."

"You're very talented. I don't know a lot about the blues, but you have a unique sound."

"Unique good or unique I-can't-think-of anything-good-to-say-so-I'll-say-unique?"

"Definitely good. Raspy good."

Savannah beamed. "Thank you. And you're wrong about the other."

"What other?"

"The blues. You know a hell of a lot about the blues."

"I do? Well, yes, now."

"No, always. Can you talk about your life? Your self? I mean, okay, you spent a very long marriage being some guy's beard, but that doesn't happen in a vacuum, you know?"

"A beard?"

"You know, the wife of a gay man who lives in a really deep closet."

"There's actually slang for it?"

"Sure. You don't know a lot about sex, do you?"

"I know it's messy."

"Okay, see, this is what I mean. You don't like sex. That's how you and your husband connected, on a really basic level. So if you think about it, it was not a bad arrangement. You each got what you needed. You just couldn't handle knowing it, right?"

"I'm not sure. What I've done is so much worse than knowing anything."

"Who really knows anything?"

"What do you mean?"

"Well, my boyfriend Dakota, right? He believes that there is nothing but thought and that we've thought all this up. Like, you thought me up on the side of the road and poof, there I was. You thought up a husband who used you as his beard so you killed him."

"This is all a lot of pseudo-philosophical malarkey."

"Oh my god, you said 'malarkey.' You are so not the type to kill a person. But anyway, here's the thing."

"I suppose I could just think him back alive, correct?"

"Well?"

"You must be crazy."

"Yeah, I am, but so is everybody—including you."

Clista's muscle memory sprang into a mode of defense that immediately fizzled. Crazy? With such a buffed and polished image? With a picture-perfect life? With the dead husband laid out across his computer desk? "Maybe I can think him back alive?"

"Damn right. It's got to be worth a freaking try."

They ate just outside the city limits at Uncle Stumpy's Bodacious Barbecue Bin, thick brown sauce crawling across their fingers, down their chins, sticky napkins piled on the tabletop. Clista found herself laughing at the mess of it all. "This is real barbecue. I've never had the real thing," and she sucked on her fingers just like Savannah did. And when Savannah flipped open her cell phone to call boyfriend Dakota to come and pick her up, Clista studied the way the young woman cocked her head, trilled her voice up and down, like a delightful little bird, as she spoke. Twenty-six, yet so much like a young girl—enthusiastic, forward looking, hopeful, on the verge of a dream.

They embraced in the parking lot. "I never knew," Clista said. "How could I not know?"

"But didn't you, really? Come on, didn't you? Way down deep? In your guts?"

Clista opened her purse and withdrew the compact and tube of coral lipstick. "I guess that's a thing to consider." She reapplied her signature color, pulled out a Kleenex and blotted a kiss onto it. She folded the Kleenex and handed it to Savannah. "If you're ever really low, give your-self a kiss from me."

"Oh, I've already been plenty low. I'm aiming for up now. But, just in case, thanks."

"You'll be okay here?" Clista glanced around the parking lot. It was not the best neighborhood, judging by the buildings in various stages of disrepair, and day had fallen into dusk.

"Oh, hell yeah. Dakota won't be too long."

"But it's getting dark and you're unfamiliar with the area." There was a pharmacy across the street that was well lit. "You should go to the bench by that drug store."

Savannah giggled. "Are you kidding? Nothing's going to happen to me. You should know this about me by now. No point in letting worry rule your world, huh?"

"I guess."

"So have you decided what you're going to do?"

"Yes, I have."

"And it feels right?"

"Yes."

"Good."

The champagne-colored Cadillac was warm from the sunlight that had been trapped inside just a short time ago—invisible but there, the traces of a star. Clista rolled down the windows and waved as she waited to pull out of the parking lot. She looked back for a few seconds longer to see Savannah arrange her possessions and plop down on her duffel bag next to the front of the rib joint, a snapshot of a reality Clista had enjoyed for a day. She wasn't sure if the woman—no, the girl—was a chance that fell out of the sky or a providential event sent by some spiritual presence in an effort to set things right. Maybe the girl really would fade from existence once Clista turned away, so she hesitated for a moment, not wanting that vibrancy to dissipate, like the rays of the sun were.

"Just go!" Savannah shouted, waving her off, laughing.

Clista giggled, a genuine sound, pressed her coral pump to the gas pedal, and pulled away. She started to roll up the windows, but caught herself, even told herself "No," right out loud. Then, at a glimpse of her eyes in the rearview mirror, she even whispered, "You crazy fucker."

And she left the windows down into the evening, rolling south through the farm country, past the scrubby towns and lives of folks left behind. The push of air blew a rhythm of comfort into her soul, disengaging strands of platinum blond that whipped about her face, growing into a small hurricane of color-treated hair spiraling around the eye of coral lips. She would drive well into the night, until she made it all the way home, consuming every millisecond with the fierce energy of thinking, thinking hard, thinking him back alive.

❧ GIRL SHOES ❧

by Lari White

I have a crush on this pair of shoes. Six-and-a-half-inch platforms
of saucy Grrrrl Power dolled up in pastel purple curlicues and peachy
yellow scrolly-doos. A strappy Summer of Love on steroids. They're
audacious—they demand attention. It's impossible to walk into a room
wearing these shoes without hearing at least one "Damn, girl! Look at
you in them shoes!" They're completely silly—they refuse to take life
too seriously. They send a shout out to a freewheeling fashion posse:
super-flared bell-bottoms, a flouncy little Chiclet of a halter top, ho-wor-
thy oversize hoops. They wouldn't give a cold shoulder to a cultured set
of pearls, but even pearls cop an attitude in the company of these shoes.
Best of all, these shoes are dangerous. And not just because you could
break your fool neck trying to walk in them. No, honey, these shoes are
likely to strut you into some edgy situations. If you work 'em right.

These shoes probably saved my life, but I don't mean that to sound
melodramatic. Melodrama is a capital offense in my family, punishable
with death by scoffing—a much more tedious method than firing squad,
but every bit as fatal. What's more, we are an intensely private tribe, so
even if there was drama—and I'm not saying there was, but if there had
been—I wouldn't be talking about it.

I found these shoes a few years ago, in Seattle visiting my baby sister,

Natasha. She's a hospice chaplain and an advocate for Mental Health Services, and her graceful daily walk with death and depression makes her the closest thing to a saint my family will ever be able to claim. I was there to help her deliver her first baby, but I was also secretly hoping to exploit her counseling skills, because I was smack dab in the middle of an extended funk, having trudged a good ways down the yellow brick road into the dark and scary forest of Life Beyond Forty, and gotten stuck right around that point where the Scarecrow says, "Now, I don't know, but I think it's going to get darker before it gets any lighter..." She, on the other hand, was nine giddy months into her first pregnancy after a long and painful battle with the Fertility Gods that she and her husband only narrowly won with the help of fervent prayer and modern technology. Thrown into this already potent emotional moment was the sad and sudden death of my husband's father, which took me from nursery to funeral home and back again in the span of a few days. I guess I was a little raw.

I was only one day back in Seattle from my father-in-law's South Carolina burial when our labor-induction walk through Seward Park opened some close-to-the-bone conversation. I started telling Natasha about the voices that had slowly been taking over in my head: mean, hateful monsters spewing endless streams of negativity. They criticized my every move, belittled every creative effort. They harassed me sleepless in the middle of the night, and started every day with their shitty chatter. Her empathy drew out the details, like someone sucking poison out of a snakebite, and I found myself speaking, voicing out loud the ugly words that had crept into and come to consume my thoughts.

I look over at the piano, longing to sit and touch the ivory keys and make up something beautiful: "You don't have time for that, Lari. Look at the house—you should be pulling out the vacuum cleaner."

I see an article about a young researcher's cancer treatment breakthrough: "Why have you so wasted your life? You could have used your mind and your talents for work that's meaningful and useful, and you've spent it on what, singing songs?"

I'm drilling multiplication facts with my homeschooled third-grader, growing ever more agitated and impatient, torturing us both because in my head I'm hearing: "You're not a teacher, Lari—who are you kidding?

As if you could give your child the best education!"

I'm asked to write my bio for the program of an upcoming show and I'm paralyzed after the first sentence: "You haven't accomplished jack, loser, what kind of BS are you going to try and spin to make it sound like you have?"

If I'm with my kids I'm "not working enough," and if I'm in the studio I'm "neglecting the kids." If I have a moment of confidence I'm "full of myself." A moment of selflessness sours into sarcasm: "Sure, I'll take care of it, I *ALWAYS* take care of it, no one else is gonna take care of it, right?"

I've always placed overmuch stock on my intelligence, what I like to think is my better-than-average thinking ability, but at that point I could honestly claim to have a mind like a steel trap—a small and brutally inescapable space I shared with murderers and thieves.

"No one cares about your so-called work, Lari, you could quit altogether and no one would even notice."

"Just shut up and go along, Lari."

"Stop trying to get attention, Lari."

"You're too old."

"You're too nice."

"You're too short."

My sweet sister, defender of all weak creatures, jumped to my psyche's side declaring, "Well, they're all just a bunch of bullies!"

Turns out she's studied a whole therapeutic technique called Voice Dialogue Therapy, a clinical process of identifying and consciously interacting with the various imagined voices that can populate one's thoughts. By the time we reached the playground we'd identified a whole gang of heinous characters taking up space in my head: the Merciless Judge, the Pusher Achiever, the Soul-Crushing Pragmatist, the People Pleaser, the Toxic Martyr, and the bad-ass bully of them all, the Critic. Turns out I'm not just crazy, I'm freaking Sally Field in *Sybil*.

Now, in the Shoe Burnin' arena of fireside yarn-spinners that makes me a lightweight. This is no story of epic loss, no revelation of a deep dark secret. My husband's demons roll their eyes at the scrawny skeletons in my closet, and I can't hope to reach the graphic and grisly bar set by the tragedies of master Suzanne Hudson. My mom and dad are both alive and mercifully healthy. They dedicated their entire lives to giving me a better childhood, a bigger world than either of them had been given. I've known the highest highs as a performer, enjoyed all the accolades and comforts of success, complete with a spotlight.

Yet here I am, questioning my sanity, and, I have to say, that is the most disturbingly messed-up sick there is.

I hear voices. I hear the sound of dreams crashing and love dying. I hear the bones of lost and limboed kin rattling behind doors, and the whisperings of family stories too true to tell. I hear the howling even through these thick walls of pride and privacy I've labored so hard to construct, and I fear, in my blackest moments, I will never silence these ghosts. I cower in corners while they rage, damning me from angry pulpits and mocking me from suicide graves.

When you realize that all you can ultimately depend on to save you is your own mind, and your own mind is the very thing you need to be saved from, the irony gets lost. It's a Hieronymus Bosch hellscape drawn by the recursive hand of Escher.

My sister has had her own conversations with these dangerous shades. We tried to laugh, but settled on crying. Then she loved me enough to ask me, "So is there a voice that you like to hear, one that makes you feel good and strong?" I had to think, because it had been a while since I'd heard that voice, but I hadn't forgotten her.

She's my Girl voice, the voice that used to have center stage in my head. She's the freckle-faced waif with stringy hair and bright eyes. She's the voice I've known the longest, the one most familiar to my heart, because she isn't a voice developed in reaction to family history or Baptist dogma or post-feminist Western culture. She's not a defense mechanism or a psychological construct.

No sir, the Girl voice was born in dialogue with my Maker, before the invention of time, long before this skinny whitegirl body was shaped to hold her. The Girl learned the art of conversation from the designer of quarks and the composer of whipporwill song. She divined her vocabulary from the writer of The Word and the Last Word and all the words in between. The Girl is connected.

The Girl knows that fairy sculptures come to life when they think you're not looking, and that a root-beer float makes an excellent breakfast.

The Girl knows where to find sunset-colored coquina shells and wild kumquats and stones that could be Cherokee arrowheads.

The Girl knows that God loves and Jesus heals, because He healed my earache right there on Granmama's couch while my cousins played tag in the watermelon patch.

It was the Girl who earned a drawerful of encouraging rejection letters from esteemed publishers of children's books before she was in the fifth grade. She read *The Hobbit* at seven and *Lord Of The Rings* at eight and nine, and spent most of her tenth year trying to master Elven calligraphy. She practiced piano with nine small fingers on the thirty-five-dollar upright in the garage, and in the winter she'd place a bowl of warm water on the bench beside her so when her hands froze she could dip them in and thaw them out to play for another fifteen minutes.

It was The Girl who spun the Ultimate Cinderella Story, where there is no stupid glass slipper, just Cinderella's beautiful voice that moves the heart of the handsome Prince as she sings softly in his ear while they dance at midnight. And he has to search the entire kingdom and listen to every out-of-tune, scraggle-throated Star Search wannabe in the land before he finally in a twist of divine fate and against all manner of evil conspiracies by the two no-can-sing wicked step-sisters hears Cinderella singing from her locked bedroom prison and demands her release and humbly asks her for her love and they live of course happily ever after as the Prince and his world-famous and much-beloved Singing Princess.

It was the Girl who giggled when I saw these shoes sitting on the clearance rack. Natasha and I had stopped at a department store on our way home from the park, to decompress from our heavy exchange with a little retail therapy. I picked up the shoes, wide-eyed, marveling at the sheer altitude, the riot of color. "Well, those are silly," said the Soul-Crushing Pragmatist. "They don't go with anything you have, and they're way too high."

I put them back. I tried on a comfy pair of Clarkes and some sturdy Keens, but I couldn't stop thinking about the silly shoes. They made me smile. "You know, Natasha is the one who really needs shoes," interrupted the Toxic Martyr. "Why aren't you looking out for her?"

I looked for running shoes for my sister, and a pair of cozy slippers, but then I found myself wandering back around by the crazy platforms, so I grabbed them and took them over to show her. One glance elicited a delighted squeal and a demand to see them on. "There's no point trying them on," the Critic said with my voice. "I'd look like an idiot in these." I put them back on the shelf again.

I tried to find something that would please everyone in the peanut gallery, but nothing satisfied, and all I could think about was that one unlikely pair of platforms.

So I tracked them down again and this time I strapped them on. I stood, towering over everything in sight, which for me is in and of itself a rare and thrilling experience. I strode across the shoe department like a runway model. A slightly drunk runway model. I was more than a little afraid I might fall and break something, but I only half-tripped once, and I think I covered it pretty well. I was still fighting an internal war over issues of taste and good sense when my sister posed the definitive question: "What does the Girl say?"

There was no doubt, and not a moment's hesitation—she wanted the shoes. She was not leaving the store without them. And so I paid for them, grinning like a kid as I swiped my MasterCard.

In a "God winks" kind of synchronicity, a few months later I discovered my new favorite movie, I ♥ Huckabees. It's quirky and raw and jumbles up the crass and the profound in the most perfectly human way. In the climactic self-revelatory scene the confused hero says, "How am I not myself? How am I not myself? How am I not myself?"

I immediately recognized this line as the perfect mantra, a mental sword I could wield against the gang of psychic thugs raging in my head. Any time I catch one of the bully voices imposing its singularly skewed reality, I just ask, "How am I not myself? How am I not myself? How am I not myself?"

Now, I suppose that in the grand tautology of things, I am me. I can't exactly be anything other than myself, whatever cast of internal characters that happens to include at the moment. And in all fairness, even the most hateful personalities in my head probably started out serving some good purpose, challenging me to do better, work harder, be kinder.

But, like the "friends of friends" someone brought to a party I once threw, they started out being helpful—mixing drinks, wiping up spills—

only to devolve into crashing boors and toxic gherms who eventually ruined the fun for everybody. Enough. I may never be able to completely rid myself of these crazy-making characters, but I do hold the keys to the asylum. I can decide: Who gets to dominate the session, Nurse Ratched or Jack Nicholson?

I have to confess, I still haven't figured out how to muzzle the Critic. He's a tough mofo. He just grabbed the microphone while I was writing that last paragraph, saying, "Who do you think you are, trying to write something good enough for a Shoe Burnin'?" I almost closed the computer and got out the vacuum cleaner. Instead, I responded with an act of pure poetry: I beat the crap out of him with my shoe.

I don't want to burn these shoes. I love these shoes. I will cry while these shoes burn. But I am by God going to burn them, because I am counting on this combustion to light a fire under my ass, to goose me into a higher state of consciousness, a plane where I am constantly and diligently on the lookout for more Girl Shoes—wilder, sillier, taller Girl Shoes. Shoot, Steve Madden has built a billion-dollar fashion empire on Girl Shoes and they are sitting on department store racks across America just begging for me to strap them on and Go Grrrrl!

So let this be a refining fire that sparks up the sky and incinerates every excuse the Critic and the Pragmatist and the People Pleaser come up with to make me sensible and small. Torch those lies! Let this flame become the hot spotlight as the Girl steps back onto center stage, making her voice heard, and working those shoes.

❧ ROCK AND ROLL SHOES ❧

by Chuck Jones

It was the year of Orwell.

I had been counting down to 1984 since I'd first heard of the book as a teenager, though I'd never actually read it. It was one of those year dates that get stuck in the public psyche, much like 1999, in which case I started partying like it was before it was, circa 1984, much earlier if I'm honest. But I didn't attribute the significance of my level of hedonism to the commensurate significance of a millennial turn until Prince put the notion in my foggy head. Oddly enough, by the time 1999 rolled around I was pretty much partied out, although I had just enough left in me to beget a lovely flower of a girl child that year. Like everyone else, for the most part I had affixed my year date attention to 2000 and the inevitability of world collapse and apocalypse brought on by the very shortsighted tendency of computer programmers to use two digit dates instead of four. We made it through that just fine. We even made it through 2012, Mayans be damned, which they were.

In 1984 I was a guitar player and singer in a rock band. As such, I was occasionally prone to purchasing flashy items for my wardrobe. To wit, one nicely turned pair of leather, multi-colored high-top tennis shoes, in the haute couture style of Chuck Taylor. I also had most of my stage jeans taken in at the inseam, because the Levi Corporation didn't seem to appreciate the stork-like physiognomy of my gorgeous gams, nor my inner need to have each and every muscle accentuated just so. I worked out and sometimes wore sleeveless T-shirts or blue-jean jackets to show off my barely bulging biceps, an unfortunate practice that I've only recently retired. It was the eighties, but I never, and I repeat, never, ever put styling gel or mousse in my hair and then blow-dried it in the upside down position with the appropriate amount of hair spray action, to attain that mile high look, à la Flock of Hairdos, that fleeting eighties band. Well, practically never, anyway.

In the sweaty, sweltering Memphis July of 1984, me and the boys had just finished four strong strutting sets of gyrating, grinding, glorious power pop/rock, replete with stage rolling, PA stack climbing and table hopping guitar solos at the Stage Stop, a redneck rock bar on the north side and pretty much home base for us at the time. We called ourselves Avenue, because that was the only thing innocuous enough for all four of us to agree on. Four grown men of average intelligence sitting around a table with a bottle of Jack Daniels topping off their iced teas trying to come up with a name for their band, one that encapsulates all their high hopes and dreams, accentuates their adolescent rock and roll bravado, and signifies their presumed undeniable sexiness, is a story in itself. We got off at midnight and decided to go to Midtown to hear some friends of ours that played in another rock combo, and to drink off some of that post show energy. It was to be one of those otherwise mundane quotidian decisions—like the time when I was only eighteen and decided to hitchhike home from work as a guitar instructor one night and got picked up by a guy my age named Phillip, probably because he saw the guitar, who invited me to a huge party at his house, and so I, never having been one to turn down a good time, went with him and partied like it was indeed 1999, and eventually he dated my next door neighbor, then dated and married my sister, while first his uncle, then his first cousin, dated a lady that lived down the street from me, whom the first cousin eventually married, divorced, and then remarried—one of those decisions, those little turns in the road we take, that wind up being a simple twist of fate with not inconsiderable consequences.

She was there, on Madison Avenue in Midtown Memphis, after midnight, in that now long gone and most misnomered of bars, The Bombay Bicycle Club. And she happened to be what would now be referred to as the BFF of the girlfriend of the guitar player in the band we were there to see, who happened to be a friend of mine. Her name was Becky, and it was only much later that I remembered the time when I was about twelve going to see a Tom Sawyer movie, featuring a particularly fetching blond playing the character of Becky, and having a premonition that I would one day grow up to marry a beautiful blond haired Becky just like her. Or maybe it wasn't a premonition, but a cognition of a parallel universe where I had been born earlier, and knew my Becky already, since according to Einstein, the past, present, and future are all existing simultaneously, and some physicists posit that our experience of time could be nothing more than the quantum matter that comprises the molecules of our infinite selves shifting through infinite other universes where we also exist. She later told me that the first thing she noticed about me was my multi-colored leather high-tops. They were blue, red, green, and yellow, and as intended, rather hard to miss. She claims that as her eyes climbed up from my fluorescent feet, over my tightly jeaned haunches, and farther and farther up, until she eventually took in my entire essence, she had the inexplicable and irresistible urge to meet me. Her BFF, who turned out to be a mere BF, told her she could forget about me, because I was dating "Lisa." Lisa worked at the local music store and was a raven-haired wisp of a thing. She had sold me a sea foam green Kramer electric guitar with a Floyd Rose whammy bar and that had led to a rather lopsided relationship, you know, one of those "couldn't wait to see me right around the time she needed help moving" kinds of relationships. She took a big leap-frog forward in guitar player boyfriends very shortly thereafter when she dumped me for Joe Walsh, who was hanging around Memphis at the time, not long after the Eagles had broken up. Becky was not deterred, and so we were introduced. The first thing I noticed about her was her beautiful smile and doleful blue eyes, framed by luxurious shocks of tumbling blond locks.

She invited me to join her a couple of nights hence at a house she was sitting for some friends, our first and last official date. She made me a steak dinner with all the trimmings and the evening turned into the early morning hours, which turned into the next day, and then the next, and then the next. Although it was about a month before she "officially" moved in with me, I don't recall us spending many nights apart after that first night. I would come home to my apartment and find little gifts sitting outside my door that she had dropped off during the day. It might be fresh baked cookies or brownies, maybe a scented candle for my apartment, or expensive, scented soaps, which, no matter how broke we were, she always insisted on buying. Becky is gonna have her fancy soap, by God, no matter what. Being on the mend and somewhat melancholy from the recent ditching by Lisa, I wasn't looking for a steady relationship, but Becky just seemed to make everything all right. She could cook, bake, sew, crochet, tat, quilt, change her own oil, and pretty much accomplish anything she put her able mind to, which was plenty. And she loved to go camping in the woods, which I hadn't done since I was a kid. She even had all of her own camping gear: a sleeping bag, tent, pots, pans, and a colorful, woven hammock that had come all the way from Mexico. Oh, the stories that hammock could tell. Soon after she moved in she went to work tailoring custom made stage jackets to go with those multi-colored high-tops. She spent hours on end behind her trusty Bernina sewing machine making me one-of-a-kind creations, with silk lapels and such. Becky was like a breath of fresh spring air on the tail end of a gale force wind. And she had a really good job, which didn't hurt none, me being a musician and all.

After three cozy years together in my one room, upstairs, five-hundred square foot Midtown Memphis apartment, I retired my rock and roll shoes to a box in the closet, bought some cowboy boots, and moved musically, metaphorically, and geographically, to Nashville, that self-proclaimed "Music City," just two-hundred miles up Interstate 40, yet a universe away from Memphis. I put down my Fender and picked up a pen. Becky, being the perennial pragmatist, picked up a job, in a music-publishing house, as it happened. Not long thereafter, we ceased living in sin and were joined in matrimony by a judge in a holy anointed apartment complex clubhouse back in Memphis, courtesy of Becky's resident Aunt Sis. But as we settled back into Nashville, in between odd jobs and fishin' the local creeks, I started writing songs. Becky, through her connections at her new job, was instrumental in helping me to make the contacts that led to my first publishing deal. She also had a major hand some years later in that 1999 begetting of a flower of a girl wonder child, whom we call Savannah Grace, a name chosen by Becky on the mere and admirable grounds that it sounded Southern.

Southern, like that blend of Irish and folk music that made its way from the hills in the east to Nashville, then onto the airwaves of the Grand Ole Opry in the 1920s. Southern, like the call and response songs of slaves who toiled in the fields beneath the lash of big cotton and evolved into Delta blues, gospel, and rhythm and blues. Southern, like that Creole gumbo of Louisiana jazz. Southern like those two kings, B.B. and Elvis. I have a framed print of a black and white photo of Elvis and B.B. King that was taken in the midst of the Civil Rights era on Beale Street in Memphis in the mid '50s, around the time I was born just a few blocks away, a stone's throw from the Mighty Mississippi. They are standing side by side, Elvis in a dark striped suit and B.B. in an all white suit. The juxtaposition of black and white is striking. I've always loved the way this picture illustrates that music flies no flag but love. It has no allegiance except to truth. Most of the blood of the Civil War was spilled on Southern soil, and mingled there with the blood that made the cotton grow and the willow weep. From all this pain came a cry to God and that cry was American music. And when Savannah Grace, now almost fourteen, opens her mouth to grace this world with even one note from her pure and pristine heart and her prodigious and powerful lungs, all of that pain pours forth, albeit wrapped in a package ever so pretty and tied with a bow of beauty. Becky's appellation was prescient and prophetic.

So when Becky and I loaded up a trailer and moved to Nashville so I could pursue country songwriting in the late eighties, I ignored my rock and roll friends who said I was "selling out," or had just plain "gone crazy." To me it was just another birthright to explore. I immersed myself in the art and craft of writing lyrics, in that reverent pursuit of "three chords and the truth." One of the first songs I wrote that was recorded by a major artist was supposed to be a duet with Aretha Franklin and Ronnie Milsap, and wound up being a duet with Ronnie Milsap and Patti LaBelle instead. It seemed that Aretha's record label couldn't come to terms with Ronnie's, whereas Patti and he shared the same label. It also seemed that although you could take the boy out of Memphis, you couldn't take Memphis out of the boy—my first major recording as a Nashville writer was a duet with a soulful blind white boy and a black soul sister. Go figure. It was a decidedly funky song called "Love Certified," and I was delighted to get to play electric guitar on the duet, which appeared on Milsap's album. Ronnie's studio was right next door to the publishing company I was writing for. Nashville was and is a small yet potent and tightly woven community of artistic types from the four corners of the globe. *Entertainment Tonight* did a piece on the duet and I was invited to this media event. I still have a picture of me and my co-writer, J.D. Martin, standing on either side of Ronnie and Patti. This was to be the first of many such functions I would attend all through the 1990s, a period of immense growth in the country music industry. It seems as though the rise of heavy metal and rap on the radio had driven a lot of mostly white Americans to seek out the country stations and as a result, country artists began to sell a lot of gold and platinum records. This was also due to the fact that country music at this time began to sound a lot like the country flavored rock and singer-songwriter artists of the 1970s that my generation had grown up with. There was a mass exodus of LA musicians to Nashville, which was by this time already the recording studio capital of the world, with more studios per capita than anywhere else. Artists like Vince Gill, who had once been a member of Pure Prairie League, became known as country artists. Indeed, Vince himself became a country superstar. Other members of country rock and rock bands of the '60s and '70s morphed into country bands of the '90s, like Exile and the Desert Rose Band.

This evolution was nothing new per se, as popular music, which country is just one form of, has always been in a state of constant flux. It's hard for some to accept this, and so they maintain a "purist" attitude, longing for things to return to the way they imagine them to have been at some perfect point in time.

So it was that the jazz of the '20s and '30s offended those of the older generation who deemed it a threat to cultural values and indicative of the decadence of the Roaring Twenties. So it was that the rock and roll of the '50s and rock of the '60s offended that older generation who saw them as a heralding of and extension of, respectively, the desegregation of society, as an aid to civil rights and the loosening of sexual mores. In both of these cases, thankfully, they were right.

I understand the human longing to have things as they were, but the past is ever clouded with the myopia of memory. And as it turns out, life was never really as good as we remember it being. The truth is that at any point in history, musical or otherwise, the purists are in denial of the fact that in their long gone perfect past, there were those pining for some even longer goner perfect past, as well as those for whom that past was not so perfect in the first place. Those who would turn back the hands of time to the post war *Leave It to Beaver* era of the 1950s, for instance, are either ignorant of the social inequities of the day, or to some extent in agreement with them.

If it weren't for black culture, and the melding of it with European culture as far back as the early nineteenth century, there would have been no blues, no ragtime, no black gospel, no jazz, no R&B, no rock and roll, no country, no soul. There would be no American music as we know it.

Both black and white music in America have a history of being equally inspired by perceived good and evil. Both were born of sinners and saints. As a child, there were two distinctly formative influences on my worldview. One was my strict disciplinarian born-again father and the other my rebellious, hell raisin' eldest brother. Dad didn't even allow us to say the word *fart*, much less let one loose, whereas David was my spirit guide into the wonderful world of profanity, the mysteries of sex, alcohol, and all things forbidden by Dad. David was also the one who brought home the first 45s I ever heard. These early records, by everyone from Ray Charles and Otis Redding to the Beatles, Jan and Dean, and Roy Orbison, were candy to my young ears. My dad was no saint, and I've never been a believer in the concept of sinners, though David would certainly have qualified, but it's not hard to guess who was gonna win that battle.

There is a wonderful illustration of this blending in the movie *The Color Purple*, where the preacher's estranged daughter, Shug Avery, is hanging out on the riverbank outside of the juke joint with her fellow revelers on a Sunday morning, singing, drinking, and having a good time. Just as Shug begins to sing the line, "Let me tell you something," they hear the strains of the choir wafting in the wind from the church just across the river, striking up the song "Maybe God Is Tryin' To Tell You Somethin'." Shug stops cold and listens, then begins to sing along with the choir, trading vocal licks with the soloist (both of them incredible gospel singers), leading the band and revelers across the river and into the church and right up to her father, where the scene culminates in an emotional hug as Shug whispers into her father's ear, "See Daddy, even sinners have soul." And father and daughter are reconciled. One of my favorite artists of all time, Ray Charles, grew up playing and singing black gospel music. Then when he began to sing sexually charged lyrics to those same infectious gospel rhythms, he received all manner of criticism. Such merging of spiritual and sensual elements is ubiquitous in American music, and for Charles it was the beginning of a long and fruitful career. Predominantly white country music has a similar historical duality, having its roots in church hymns as well as honkytonks. And whether my toe was tapping in those multi-colored high-tops or well-worn cowboy boots, I've always embraced this musical and cultural heritage, regardless of whether it was a hallelujah to the heavens or a dance with the demons.

The Grand Ole Opry forbade the use of drums on stage for decades, perhaps an unconscious echo of the forbidding a century before of slaves from playing drums or percussion instruments of any kind. Even though Bob Wills defied the Opry edict as early as 1944, it wasn't until 1973, when the Grand Ole Opry moved from the Ryman Auditorium to Opryland, that a full drum set was allowed on stage.

In the 1960s, producers like Owen Bradley and Chet Atkins began adding strings and other pop influences to country records, creating what was called the "Nashville Sound," which led to greater and greater crossover success for country artists on the pop charts. Purists objected. And in the late '70s and early '80s, the Urban Cowboy craze, against the purists' cries, once again injected country music with pop influences, just prior to a traditional resurgence in the mid '80s with the emergence of artists like Reba McEntire, George Strait, and Randy Travis. Then came the '90s and the continued infusion of rock and pop influences into country music, which with very few alternatives on pop radio, led to the white exodus to country music that I previously described, giving me a career in the process. Nowadays, if it weren't for the steel guitar or fiddle in the mix, you'd be hard pressed to know whether you were listening to a country music station or a rock station.

When I was a boy there was much musical diversity in America, most of which could be heard on the same local radio station. There were only two or three chart genres in the musical trades. These days, there are dozens of chart genres, yet an increasing homogenization of the music itself, black and white. And thanks to decreasing regulation by the FCC during the Clinton years, two or three corporations have bought up all of the local radio stations.

My earliest musical memories are of a little white church in rural Arkansas, about an hour west of Memphis. My folks had met in Louisville, Kentucky, where they both earned college degrees, Dad at the Southern Baptist Theological Seminary and Mom at the Women's Missionary Union Training School, which was located on the seminary's campus. Mom took the same courses from the same teachers, but was not allowed the Bachelor of Divinity Degree that my dad received. She earned a Masters in Religious Education instead. Mom had gone to Louisville in hopes of going to medical school, as she had previously majored in pre-med, but soon learned that as a woman there was no way for her to become a legal resident in Kentucky without either first getting married, or her parents moving there. She had no legal rights. This was after she had been denied acceptance at Baylor University on the grounds that out of an entering class of two hundred only two were allowed to be women. This was the 1950s that some folks would have us return to, for reasons I have never been able to fathom. Mom was obviously no June Cleaver.

Mom and Dad met each other while volunteering as Sunday school teachers at the Central Baptist Mission and were married about a year later. Both dreamed of being missionaries to Africa but Arkansas was as close as they ever got, supposedly because of Dad's ulcer. The little white church I'm recalling was not their first, as the Southern Baptists had early on excommunicated my dad on account of his inviting black folks to his white Baptist country church and preaching a pro integration message. My memories are of the church Daddy had built after. It was non-denominational and started out in a tent. I have pictures of the groundbreaking, and pictures of Daddy washin' folks in the blood and the mud of the nearby St. Francis River, a holdover from his Southern

Baptist training, all of which would be eventually undone. This was long before he wrote a book about Jesus and organized religion called *The Rock Of Offense*. This was before he wrote a book about Paul and called him a liar. This was before his nervous breakdown (probably due to a long overdue grieving of his own mother's suicide, when he was only ten) which he always called his "breakthrough," because of its culmination in a walk in the woods, where he had a spiritual epiphany: a terrible weight lifted from his shoulders at the exact moment he said, "Satan, get thee behind me!" It was at that moment he says he realized it was the church that had been wrong all along, not him. He came to view the Christian church, in all its myriad denominations, as an abomination, turning Jesus' pacifistic admonition to "turn the other cheek" upside down one minute, and the sword he brought into the peace on earth he came not to bring the next.

Mama played piano and Daddy preached and led the choir in hymns like "The Old Rugged Cross." She would lay my little sister and me on a patchwork quilt underneath the window where the Sunday morning sun shone through, right next to the piano. And at times a chiaroscuro would fall across my face, across the room and across the pulpit Daddy had built out of oak with his own hands and inlaid with a cross. I don't know why, but in all my memories of this period of my young life the sun is always shining, though I know it must've rained plenty.

My brother recently took Dad for a drive out of Memphis and down those Arkansas back roads to the place where the old church, Boatrun Church, as it was called, after the spot on the St. Francis River near where it sat, used to be. We have visited it every decade or so for a while now and the last time I went out, about fifteen years ago, the original building was still there, but had been added on to. My brother said there was still a church there this time, but it was not the same building. There was a man mowing the grass. Turned out he was also the current pastor. After learning Dad was the one who had established a church on that site in the 1950s, he gave them the grand tour. The original building, the one I have photos of them breaking ground for, had burned to the ground a few years back. On approaching the altar, my brother realized that the pulpit was the same one Dad had built all those years ago. It had never been replaced in the sixty years since, and was the one thing spared in the fire. Don't ask me how. It didn't have a charred spot on it. It was the same pulpit from whence I first heard about David and Goliath and them pesky Philistines. The fishes and the loaves and the woman at the well. The raisin' up of Lazarus and Peter denying Jesus thrice before the cock's crow. The sermon on the mount, where Jesus made the ten commandments even tougher. And where the King James version and my own daddy told me I had to hate my mother and my father, my brother and my sister, my husband and my wife, son and daughter, and deny them like he denied his, if I really loved Jesus. The pulpit where I was told that if I wanted to follow him I'd have to take up my own cross. I decided to take up a Stratocaster instead.

I was born into a world of clearly demarcated black and white—we couldn't pray together, eat together, ride together, be together, couldn't even drink from the same water fountain. It seemed that only in the world of music had these lines been obliterated, and miscegeny fully embraced, creatively at least (not to gloss over the fact that black artists and writers were routinely robbed of their royalties). Perhaps that's one reason that from an early age I knew I was destined to be a musician.

When we moved from Arkansas to Memphis in 1960 I began to soak up all of those sounds emanating from Sun and Stax, and then later American and High Studios. I also loved the Motown sound and the Beatles and the British Invasion as well. My heroes tended to be pickers like Eric Clapton, Jimi Hendrix, Jeff Beck, and Jimmy Page. Ironically, I heard much of the music that was first created in the Delta, right down the road from where I grew up, for the first time via British rockers who were influenced by black American blues artists. My folks used to say I was the only one in the family who inherited its musical genes. As a young man, my dad's father had played fiddle and traveled around the countryside with a vocal quartet, playing mostly churches. My mother's dad had played a chromatic harmonica, which I inherited when he died in 1964. But both of these men had lived in tougher times, eking out their existence from the hard-scrabble earth, with music being only a sideline or a solace to pass a summer's night on the front porch or sitting in the yard beneath the wishin' stars. Neither of them still played by the time I came along. But wherever it comes from, I'm eternally grateful for whatever made music my passion. I've heard it said that if you find something you love, and do that, you'll never work a day in your life. For the most part I've found this to be true. And now my own daughter, Savannah Grace, appears to be drinking from that same well, drawing from that same gene pool. Born and raised in Nashville, when she opens her mouth to sing, Memphis comes out. Lately she's taken to singing a few songs from the black and white days, from the seminal days, before I donned my multi-colored high-tops, songs by artists like Etta James, James Brown, and Aretha Franklin. That music still holds up, still rings true, and I believe it always will. When Becky and I made the move all those years ago, I wasn't leaving Memphis behind, I was bringing it with me.

And this Memphis boy fit right into the burgeoning music Mecca that was Nashville in the late '80s. Those cowboy boots, somewhat ill-fitting at first, began to get broken in. They eventually got downright comfortable from all those walks to the mailbox, as my songs began to show up on the radio dial and on gold and platinum records. But after all these years and all that ink under the bridge, that muddy Mississippi—where I was baptized in the blues and where Becky and I sat on a blanket on its banks not so long ago, watching the sunset over Arkansas turn fields of cotton into fields of gold—still springs silently from my heart, its rapids roaring through my soul, its tributaries rushing through my veins and coursing through my capillaries. Yes, after all these years, my heart still beats the blue, red, green, and yellow of those old leather high-tops.

If only I could remember just where in the hell I put them.

A RED CORVAIR AND
BLACK AND WHITE WINGTIPS
by Michael Reno Harrell

It was a red 1964 Corvair two door. Good on gas, seated four, easy
to park and Ralph Nader's theories on unsafe at any speed be damned.
This was a General Motors product, for God's sake. My dad had spotted it sitting at the graveled edge of the parking lot of the Sunset Shell
station out on the west end of town. The guy who fixed flats and washed
cars down there was selling it for his uncle or cousin or somebody. Anyway, the shoe polish lettered cardboard sign stuck under the driver's side
wiper blade read, "Good Transpatason $275."

My dad had seen the old bucket driving home from work one Friday
evening, and a seed had been planted. Unbeknownst to my mom, my
father was considering buying a second car so that he wouldn't have to
drive my mother to the Crescent Center Super Market every week and
follow her up and down the aisles while she mulled over the two-cent
difference in the price of a loaf of Bunny bread as opposed to Sunbeam.
Dad wasn't a shopper. Or patient.

And as a bonus, my mother could drive my brother and me to
school, thus relieving my father of that chore as well, which would allow
him to eat breakfast at the Little Dutch Restaurant with the movers and

shakers of our little burg and perhaps get the chance to move and shake a bit on his own.

Dad had joined the navy back before the war to learn a trade, and he had, steam turbine operation and maintenance. This vocation was very much in demand if you happened to live aboard a ship. There were, however, very few ships plying the rivers of east Tennessee after he returned to civilian life. It turned out that the only job my father was qualified for was at the local rayon plant in their coal-fired power facility. Tapping the glass face of a boiler's pressure gauge several times an hour and penciling the reading onto a ruled form was somehow not very fulfilling either monetarily or mentally for Dad.

He had tried art school by mail having been advised that he had a natural talent for the craft after drawing the pirate on a matchbook cover and mailing it in to Art Instruction, Inc., in Minneapolis, Minnesota. Unfortunately, it turned out that there wasn't much of a market for cartooning in east Tennessee at that time either.

Then, by chance one Saturday afternoon while sitting in the air conditioned comfort of Congress Barber Shop, he happened on an opportunity that he couldn't believe he had overlooked for so many years. Taxidermy. Just as Mark Blazer was flapping the previous customer's freshly clipped hair from his barber's cape and calling out, "Next?" Dad glanced down at an open copy of *Field & Stream* and there it was. "Learn Taxidermy at Home." What sportsman who has bagged a trophy bass or deer or squirrel wouldn't want to display his prize in the home? After sending in the tuition and receiving his spiral-bound, plastic-laminated set of instructions, he was hot to get started on his new career.

The course started with game fish, so the first thing one needed was, of course, a fish to mount. No problem. We lived in the land of TVA. There were lakes covering roughly a third of the Tennessee River Valley so there were fish and fishermen by the boatload. However, finding a fisherman willing to donate a prize bass to some idiot hanging around the local boat dock turned out to be the rub. Dad, not wanting to waste time on less than an award winning largemouth, decided to move directly on to mammals.

Having neither the weaponry nor the will to go out and dispatch his own prey, finding a candidate for mounting again turned out to be a problem. When my brother, Eddie, mentioned the possibility of the family going on a road kill expedition, Mother's foot came down, and that was the end of the taxidermy business.

One Wednesday night after prayer meeting at the church, one of the deacons, Buzz Whitely, met Mom and Dad at the door and invited them to a party. It was a gathering to sample the health and economic benefits of cooking the modern way with the stainless steel clad Health-wear Cooking System. We bought the BIG set and Dad was enrolled as a marketing trainee. After several home demonstrations which ended in what could only be described as culinary suicide, Dad wound up giving his $675 demonstration kit to my Uncle Harold and Aunt Mattie as a twenty-fifth wedding anniversary gift. Aunt Mattie graciously thanked my father and went right on cooking in her cast iron skillets and aluminum pots, and the Healthwear Cooking System was used to feed Big Sally, Aunt Mattie's old Guernsey heifer her corn and somewhere around twenty yard cats their daily ration of table scraps.

Not to be deterred, Dad was confident that he was on the right track. He was convinced that marketing was to be his future. He just hadn't found the right product. All he needed was to follow the money, as they say nowadays. And who had plenty of money? Why, the rich. And what do the rich spend their money on? Furs.

Several periodicals of the time professed (in ads) that chinchilla ranching was making millionaires of savvy working folks all over the country. And the little buggers procreated faster than rabbits. All one needed was a healthy breeding pair, and within a few months sumptuous little weasel pelts would be piling up by the bushel. Soon Dad had built racks along both walls of our little garage to support the dozens of wire cages that were to hold our furry cash crop. When our prize pair arrived they were dubbed Elizabeth and Charles and were placed on one of Mom's old cashmere sweaters which had been attacked by a swarm of moths the previous winter. Who would have thought that a little carbon monoxide from just a few minutes of warming up the car would have such a devastating effect on a couple of rodents?

Oh well. Dad wasn't one to give up. He was convinced that his natural gift was in getting others to bend to his will. Eventually.

Still, after fourteen years of marriage and several unsuccessful attempts at home marketing, he was unsure of just how to approach my mother on any deal involving the insertion of a minus sign in the bankbook. It turned out that Mom had been mulling over the best way to approach Dad on the very same subject, so when he got up the nerve to suggest that our lives sure would be simpler if Mom had her own car, the proposal was praised as brilliant. It took him several minutes to get his mouth to close.

His idea of acquiring this new conveyance was shaping up to be what these days one might refer to as a win/win situation for not only Mom and Dad but Eddie and me as well, in that riding anywhere in a car with my father was, to say the least, a trying experience, again patience not being his strong suit. I will say that our young vocabularies developed considerably along the bluer veins of the English language from our morning commutes through what was referred to as rush hour in 1980 small town east Tennessee, where no one but our father knew jack shit about the operation of a motor vehicle. The horn ring of our Chevy had developed a permanent swag from what amounted to several years' worth of accumulated pressure from my dad's big right fist. At times the hooting of the twin horns didn't satisfy his need to enlighten the idiots that he had to deal with on the road, so Dad would insert the thumb and middle finger of his left hand into his mouth and proceed to produce a piercing whistle that may be the reason for the tinnitus I suffer from to this day.

His second car idea having finally scored a homer with my mom, the following Saturday morning Dad loaded me, brother Eddie and Mom into the family car and off we went to check out the Corvair before minds got changed. We parked the Biscayne and Eddie and I jerked open our doors and flew over to where the little compact sat on its four mismatched tires—although the two on the driver's side were whitewalls, the front being a Goodyear and the rear a Goodrich. Close enough.

Within seconds of our arrival my brother had informed me that this was a cool car. Being a teenage boy, of course, gave him all the authority needed to make such a pronouncement. And being the younger brother of same gave me every reason to concur.

Dad advanced on the car like it might be harboring a family of copperheads or a swarm of yellow jackets. He circled the thing first from about thirty feet out then closed in slowly. Mom already had her hands cupped to the passenger side glass and was studying the upholstery, not so much for wear as for color and texture. The original seat covers appeared to have once been red and white. That was pure conjecture based on the fact that the seats were now more pinkish and gray with carefully placed accents of black electrician's tape in the high wear sections of the fabric. The driver's seat back was covered with a safety-pinned, rose-patterned K-Mart bath towel. I knew the origins of the seat cover because we had its mate hanging from the chrome bar in our own bathroom.

Mother stepped back and allowed, "That will have to go. Florals have no place in an automobile." Mother had an eye for décor. When my father discovered that he had a talent for Paint By Number horse heads, my mother refused to display them in the living room. Even as a young boy, I could appreciate her taste.

Forget seat coverings, if this thing had been a Model T with rusted running boards and a straight backed chair for a seat, Mom would have taken it. She was on the verge of getting her own car! Of course, Eddie and I were ecstatic. I mean, a Corvair was almost a Corvette. Right?

The wash guy noticed us all peeking in windows and kicking tires and wandered out, drying his hands on a greasy shop rag. "She's a beauty, ain't she?" he said. "Only showing 43,000 on the odometer," with the emphasis on "showing."

Since any quoted price for any vehicle is nothing more than a starting point for negotiation, Dad opened with, "So, how much are you thinking it would cost for a person to take this basket case off your hands?" The dealing escalated, or perhaps descended, from there. Eddie and I were somewhat fascinated with this serve-and-return bantering until Mom offered to spring for Nehi peach sodas, at which point the dealing took a back seat to refreshments.

Mom took the only chair in what could loosely be described as the lounge area of the station while Eddie and I went out front and stomped on the bell hose until the owner threatened to feed us to the one-eyed German shepherd chained to the bumper of the Sunset Shell wrecker parked around the side. Mother was too busy pretending to read a tire recapping manual while keeping an eye on the parry and thrust taking place a few yards beyond the plate glass window to even notice that her offspring were being completely obnoxious in a public place. On any other occasion, this would have been a totally unthinkable situation, punishable by a smart ear pinch followed later by the much harsher withholding of slices of chocolate cake. But there is something about crashing a Converse All-Stared heel against a rubber hose and hearing that clang that is irresistible to an adolescent male. At sixty-four years of age I still grin at the thought of such.

Meanwhile, outside, Dad would throw his hands high into the air and shake his head as he turned and walked back towards our car while the wash guy would pat the hood of the Corvair and coo about the sense of economy that a man of my father's intelligence must possess to even be considering such a gas sipper.

At this point my father would slowly turn and study the little car, head cocked to one side and his arms crossed over his chest. Slowly his right hand would rise to his jaw and the fingers of that hand would begin to stroke the cleft of his chin. After a few moments of deliberate study, Dad would drop his arms to his sides and shrug. His face would then contort into a rather pained expression of uncertainty and he would utter a figure that would have the wash guy slapping his forehead and shaking his head as if a Junebug had just flown into his ear. At which point the whole scenario would repeat. This went on for so long that for a diversion Mom bought Eddie and me each a pack of Lance peanut butter and cheese crackers with supper looming just a hopeful half hour away.

After the smoke had finally settled, by God we rode home in the Corvair, Mom, Eddie, and me all on that front bench seat, the radio blasting and the three of us reveling in our new found freedom, trailing a not so faint cloud of blue which settled across most of east Tennessee. Mom had learned to drive on an A model Ford, so a three speed on the floor was old hat to her. She would rev away from a traffic light in first, then yell, "Shift!" and I would move my left knee around the shifter as Mom slid her into second.

We absolutely loved that little car. It carried us to Friday night football games and Monday night Boy Scout meetings and to Sunday school when Dad had what Mom referred to as the "twelve ounce flu." It got on just fine with vice-grip window cranks, recapped rubber and reclaimed 30-weight motor oil. And three dollars worth of regular would keep the little mill turning a week and more. It managed with baling wire muffler hangers and looked great with its new set of red and white J.C. Whitney hounds tooth seat covers.

Eddie learned to drive in that Corvair and when Dad finally bought Mom the Nova, the little car went to Eddie. I remember the day he left with what looked to be a moving van load of stuff packed inside the little jewel for his freshman year at the University of Tennessee. We all hugged him and Mom sat a brown paper Crescent Center Super Market bag of her fried chicken and two loaves of Bunny bread on top of the two suitcases there on the passenger seat as he pulled out onto David Avenue. The Corvair carried him safely past Jefferson City, the Four Way Inn, and across the Holston River before it sadly gave up the ghost just two miles shy of Melrose Hall men's dorm. Dad sent the Sunset Shell wrecker all the way down there to Knoxville and had the carcass towed back and parked in the back yard of our house, where it spent the next seven years under a tarp.

A neighbor boy, Butch MacIntyre, used to come over every day after school and try to talk my dad into selling him the hulk. Dad finally agreed that if Butch could get the thing running he could have it for a dollar. The boy pulled the little six banger out and replaced the cracked head right there on our patio. Butch wound up driving the Corvair to the University of Arizona for the whole time it took him to obtain his degree in engineering and then to Alaska, where he still lives and works today. He gave the car to his cousin who drove it as far back as Seattle, where it was stolen.

Screw Ralph Nader. As I said, Dad hit a homer when he bought the Corvair and a whole lot of us got to round the bases with him.

My father finally did find his calling. Twice over the next several years he made and lost what most folks would deem a fortune in real estate through shear tenacity and a dogged belief in himself. It turns out that he really did have a knack for selling, just no head for business. Lots of i's and t's got neglected. Thing is, he never lost that confidence in himself. And he never looked back, just kept looking for that next deal that would put him back in the game. He drove lots of fine cars and clunkers over many up and down years. He ran with the big dogs in some pretty big races and watched the pack disappear down the trail more than a few times. Finally the dice turned cold and the years clouded his brain, until his world became the size of a room in a vinyl-sided facility with bad art on the walls and wire on the windows. Who knows, maybe somewhere in that old noggin he hit it big one more time.

And me, I spent most of my life looking for what I didn't find—not for a long, long time. It sure wasn't a career in sales. I knew from the time I tried hawking Boy Scout popcorn to friends, neighbors and even loved ones that marketing wasn't my strong suit.

I loved music, but wasn't a talented guitarist. Not like so many of those guys who could really play. I could carry a tune, but I didn't know how to connect with an audience. I guess that was on account of my lack of salesmanship. Oh, I did my time in bars singing John Prine and Jimmy Buffett covers and was as good at that as most of the boys who sit on stools and pound out the hits of the talented.

I tried writing country songs in Nashvegas for a couple of years back in the late '80s. That went okay as long as I was co-writing with someone who knew how that world worked, but it didn't take me long to figure out that I wasn't cut from that cloth either. I have welded pipe, been a river boat pilot, a sign painter, a carpenter, washed trucks, and delivered newspapers. And I wasn't worth much or very fulfilled for very long at any of them. Through all those years I kept going back to music, hoping to find something down that path. Not that I was making a living carrying around a guitar case, but it fed more than my carcass when times got thin.

Unlike my father's search, it was like I was traveling on a road I didn't choose, like I wasn't in the driver's seat. I kept looking down all these alleys that always seemed to run into brick walls. I wasn't miserable in any sense of the word, just getting kind of tired of bumping into brick.

Low tide hit when we lost Mom. She was in her car on the way to have lunch with friends when her world was stopped from turning by a young man in a Toyota pickup. Even the guitar couldn't rub any salve on that wound. It lay under the bed for almost three years. Then one morning, for some unknown reason I woke up with some words screaming in my head. The only way to stop the screaming was to try to drown it out with the guitar. Somehow the two melded into a song, a real song.

I played that song for a woman I had met. She didn't even know that I owned a guitar much less that I had for longer than I had owned a driver's license. With her encouragement, I found that I had a whole lot of songs dammed up in my head. These weren't songs for country music stars to record, not that any of them would have been interested. These were my songs.

That woman is now my wife and my manager. That song became the title song of my first CD. Fourteen CDs and about two hundred shows a years later, I have to say that I found my road. Believe me, I know how lucky I am. A whole world of people wind up traveling down roads they didn't choose.

I remember one Saturday morning way back there when Eddie was at Philmont Scout Ranch out in New Mexico and Dad was off in the big car on a weekend seminar down in Chattanooga, something to do with Dale Carnegie, and Mom and I went grocery shopping in the Corvair. As we drove past the Bi-Lo gas station, there at the edge of the parking lot stood a sad looking scarecrow of a fellow holding the first homeless placard that I can ever remember seeing.

The man was dressed in a threadbare suit and a pair of old black and white wingtip shoes that must have had more miles on them than the Corvair did. He looked right at us as we passed and I remember saying to Mom, "Look at that old bum. He ought to get a job so he could buy some decent shoes at least. Looks like he shops at the Salvation Army store."

Mother took her right hand off the wheel, something she normally only did to shift gears, and laid it softly on my shoulder. She shook her head slowly and said, "Son, you don't know what has caused that man to be out here in his Salvation Army shoes."

Salvation Army suit
Salvation Army shoes
Standing by the Bi-Lo
With a cardboard sign that read
Someday this could be you
In Salvation Army shoes

I ain't no bum I ain't no pilgrim
Just a traveler on a road I didn't choose

Someday you may have to leave
Your family and your home
I hope you never do
Or wear Salvation Army shoes

Here's to finding your road.

CAPO
by Wendy Reed

"A capo is a crutch, for cowards, those who don't want to learn how to play in every key."

— *Chris Clifton*

Music Is…
"A higher revelation than all Wisdom and Philosophy."

— *Ludwig van Beethoven*

"The only truth."

— *Jack Kerouac*

Usual Crane called it the road to nowhere, but it was really County Road 22. The only people who ever turned down it on purpose worked at the No. 2 furnace with his dad. Usual hated iron furnaces; they ate people alive. Who wants to go nowhere and then die? Not Usual. He and his guitar were doing fine in the lean-to. Summer's end was two months off and he would not be rushed about his future.

Usual squinted against the sun. He couldn't make out the car but saw it was stopping. The driver's door opened and someone got out. Usual pulled his cap down lower and watched as the trunk was raised. Life with his dad wasn't exactly a picnic but at least he'd never broken down on train tracks. The figure got back in the car and pulled forward but then backed right up again. The trunk waved like a stiff flag but didn't close. Stopping on the tracks was no accident. Crazy, Usual thought. Could be one of those suicides. He'd never seen a suicide. He dragged his lawn chair through the army blanket that served as his door and plopped down in front of the sheets of plywood. Now that he'd fortified the nylon weaving with electrical tape, he could plop without worry, but he was still careful when he shifted his weight. The figure went back to the trunk and then disappeared behind the passenger's side. Usual stood up but he still couldn't see any better. He moved out from the trees into the open.

Everything was quiet in these parts unless a train was coming. Even the thick walls of trees were no match for that whistle. Luckily the conductor only blew it once as it approached the crossing. Otherwise, the bit of woods he now called home was peaceful. The crows ould get annoying, but compared to the cussing fits of his dad, they were nothing. The figure didn't reappear. He moved his chair farther out into the open, toward the road's gravel shoulder. Still no figure. He thought about calling out but he didn't. Instead he chewed at a stubborn hangnail.

The silence didn't last. "Shit!" he heard. "Shit! Shitshit! SHITSHIT-SHIT!" The voice sounded female. The figure reappeared. Now he was close enough to see the figure was a female. A small one at that.

"Hey you," she called. He'd been spotted. She flapped her arms and called again. "Hey you."

Usual would have shrugged and made her come to him had he not felt the vibration in the chair's aluminum arm rests. A train was coming. It was a good ways off yet, but it was coming.

He rushed his legs up so fast that the bottoms of his feet stung. "Train's coming," he shouted. Her hair was wadded into a red clip on the back of her head sorta like a rooster. She cocked her hands on her hips. "I got the fucking jack under the damn car but can't get the shitty thing to go up for hell's bells."

He stopped a few feet from her. She didn't look like someone who would have that disease, the one that made you cuss every other word. But if he'd learned nothing else from seventeen years of living under the roof of "Superintendent Crane," as was spelled out and stitched over the shirt pocket of each uniform since last year's promotion, though the abbreviation would have been cheaper, looked better, and meant the same according to Mother, Usual had learned that looks could be deceiving.

"Pull on over, out of the train's way, and I'll change it for you."

She raised one eyebrow and tilted her head like a dog might if it was smelling something.

"Off the tracks," he said slowly, thinking maybe she had some kind of communicable problem.

"I don't hear no train," she said, as if she were insulted.

That's when he saw the kids in the back seat. The girl, maybe four or five, Usual guessed, had white-blond hair and red sucker all over her mouth. She smiled, waved the white sucker-stick toward Usual, and stuck it up her nose. The other one, either a boy or a bald girl, was asleep in a car seat.

"Lady, you've got to get this car off the tracks. A train's coming."

Car was a generous term. Most of it was an old Toyota Celica hatchback. The hood, though, had belonged on a VW beetle at one time. Someone had flattened it out so that it covered up the right side of the engine, but the left side was a grid of duct tape.

"You one of those clairvoyants, are you? The kind that knows what's coming? Then you tell me what else is coming my way. Ain't it enough that I've packed up my babies, left Jayroe, and hit a deer already?" She shaded her eyes with her hand. Glanced down the tracks, and knelt down in front of the jack. "I don't see no train but I have seen that men like to lie." She poked at the jack. It was upside down. "As good as a Michelin, my ass," she said as she put her finger into a six inch slit that didn't look accidental. He realized one of the straps on her sundress was coming untied. "I'm right about trusting God only." She wadded the hem of her dress and wiped her hands until Usual thought she'd rubbed a hole.

The train whistle blew; it was distant, but undeniable. She looked past Usual and chewed on her lip. She pulled a cigarette that must have been from behind her ear and took a drag. It was lit. She held it out to Usual. He shook his head no.

"Listen lady, all's it is, is a flat tire. Just crank it back up and drive a few more feet and we'll get it changed." She threw the cigarette down and rubbed it with her flip-flop. Her toenails had been painted once, years ago from the looks of what was left. Usual's mom would have called the color hussy red.

"You ain't got much time."

She looked at him as if he was interrupting something and then cleared her throat as if she was about to explain something to him, but then she sighed and without a word opened the passenger door and climbed across the console, sliding beneath the steering wheel to turn the key. Nothing happened. The motor didn't even turn over.

"Try it again," Usual said.

He watched her turn the key. Still nothing.

The train whistled. That meant it was down near Mud Creek's Crossing.

This time it was Usual who said, "Fuck."

"I told Jayroe this car was a piece of shit. I told him I'd get me a real car, maybe one of those Cadillacs, when I made it big. You watch. I will. I'll get me a car that cranks right up, one that won't get flat tires. I'm telling you. I've had enough. Enough. Enough. Enough." She emphasized each word with a slap to the steering wheel. He recognized the look that boiled up in her eyes and expected her to start screaming and cussing. Instead, she leaned forward like she might be melting or maybe even was going flat herself, until the steering wheel pressed into her forehead and stopped her. " I'm tired of it, plum tired. Tired tired tired of this shit shit shit."

A flat tire or, for that matter, a deflating woman, Usual could handle. But now that she was making strange sounds, he wanted to turn around and disappear into his woods. She'd probably start all that crying stuff before he knew it. Then there'd be snot and gnashing of teeth. Just the thought of it wearied him. He'd moved out here to play his guitar in peace and quiet. This was feeling decidedly unpeaceful.

So what if she was tired. He was tired, too. He chewed at a cuticle. Her sounds were really starting to get on his nerves. He didn't owe her anything. He didn't know her. He could turn around, go back into his lean-to, and smoke the last of a joint. He had enough going on without this. He needed a direction for his future, not a train wreck. At summer's end, his dad had arranged for him to get on at the furnace. By then, he needed to show that he had another option. He didn't have time to be saving some stupid woman and her kids' asses. The little girl waved at him and smiled. She had removed the sucker stick from her nose and now rammed her finger into a nostril. The way she was straining he half expected to see it come out her ear.

"Let me try," he said, as though he might turn the key more effectively. But then the train whistle blew again. It was closer than he expected. It was moving faster than a freight. Rarely did passenger trains travel through but then again, odd was becoming the day's theme.

"Get the kids out and I'll push it off. "

"Come on Forsythia," she said to the girl. But the little girl didn't raise her head. She didn't even move. She made a fart sound with her lips.

Although every single movement took forever, she managed to get herself and the little girl out and then she led the little girl by the hand over to a sprawling patch of clover that bloomed like a blood bruise at the road's edge. They both sank into the red. He guessed he'd have to get the other one. He reached in before he realized the baby was stark naked. It was definitely a boy. Four different straps and a buckle prevented Usual from removing him. The buckle wouldn't release so Usual began tugging at the straps.

"What the hell you doing?" came from behind. "You're young but I didn't take you for stupid. Don't you see he's asleep? I sure as shit don't need more years of bad luck."

Who was she to call him young? He couldn't tell how old she was but she was not old enough to be his mother. He wasn't sure she was old enough to be anyone's mother. What did she mean anyway by the whole sleep thing and luck? Mirrors and black cats were bad luck; sleeping babies, according to Mrs. Slidell, were angels. Mrs. Slidell knew a thing about luck; she'd managed to tend the nursery for as long as he could remember and so had never once had to sit through a single sermon.

Wings would be good about now. A few strong flaps and maybe this whole predicament would be over. He tried to imagine the baby with little feather wings or the pipe cleaner kind from bible school but a pain shot up the back of his calf and suddenly the wings turned into those of a pterodactyl, thin and stringy, and more fitting when its mother might just be the devil. She'd kicked him in the exact spot where a piece of tin had sliced into his Achilles tendon at Home Depot. Someone had pushed a flat cart into the line behind him and run off to get something else. The cart hadn't stopped until the sheet of razor-sharp tin hit his leg. He was in shorts and some old Birkenstocks, so there were no pants or socks to soak up the blood. Before he knew it, all the stuff for his lean-to was loaded for him and he was pulling out of the parking lot sporting a bandage from his knee down that was wrapped in such a way that it reminded him of a small armadillo. He also still had the cash in his wallet that he'd been going to use to pay for the lean-to materials. It was right next to a brand new plastic gift card the manager had given him. It was good for a hundred dollars, no expiration date whatsoever.

He ignored the pain and tried the first buckle again. It had a red push button thing that he pushed and poked every which way but it didn't give. He felt another sharp pain.

"You deaf?" she asked, as if he was the crazy one. Then her voice developed an edge. "Do. Not. Wake. Beauregard!" She kicked Usual a third time with what he guessed was her big toe, and this time it hurt. He was going to have to either slug this lady and then play Houdini to get the baby out or just push the car off the tracks with the baby inside. Pushing seemed easier.

He slammed the door. "You get the right side."

He lowered his shoulders and placed his hands on the taillight. She had not moved.

"I said get on the other side," he yelled. He heard himself and was surprised. It was loud enough that it could've been his father.

She sauntered into position like they had all day. "I bet your mama would be ashamed of you, speaking to a lady like that," she said, all puffed up as if she was on stage above him. Even the clapping of her flip-flops sounded like applause as she took her position.

"On three," Usual said. "ONE…TWO…THREE."

The train came into sight as they pushed, but Usual tried to stay focused on the car. It rocked a little but it didn't roll at all.

"Again," he called. The car lurched forward but again it rocked right back into place.

Empty coal trains were fast and they switched tracks as they headed to Pumpkin Center. He could never tell by their sounds if they were empty but sometimes, depending on the angle of the sun, he could make out the heaping coal against the horizon. He squinted until everything went black but couldn't make out a single detail.

"Harder," he yelled.

Still the car remained on the tracks.

The woman raised up gingerly, like she might break, and rubbed her lower back. "I can't push no harder. Jayroe said women are designed to take," and she stopped to look him over before deciding to continue, "a particular kind of pounding." She jabbed herself a few times with her thumb. "But I'll tell you one thing, it sure hurts like something's cracked." She pulled another cigarette from somewhere and put it in her mouth. This one wasn't lit.

Usual pushed with everything he had. Over and over he pushed and pushed, until he felt his stomach churn. The woman threw her hands up, walked over to the girl, and sat down. "You can do it, you can do it, you can," she called, with the distinct rhythm that suggested she had once been a cheerleader. Usual couldn't believe his eyes. They were making clover jewelry like it was the only thing in the world.

Even when his father was in the middle of a fit, Usual had never wanted to punch him. Right now he wanted nothing else but to smack the lady upside her head. Any mother who sat in the grass while a train was about to plow into her baby deserved it. He would give it to her, right after he got the car off the tracks. If he could still move, that is. Something in his back spasmed. The car wasn't budging. Every atom in his being began to ache.

He'd never been much on praying. Unlike his father, he didn't think *dammit* was God's last name. Usual even knew the Lord's Prayer by heart. But who didn't. It had debts and bread in it but nothing about babies and trains. He should have brought the knife with him. Maybe he should have stayed in Scouts. He needed something to cut the baby loose. He had nothing in his pockets but a roach clip. An Eagle Scout would not have this problem. Maybe he had time to run get the knife. He looked at the train. There wasn't time for that. He closed his eyes and the Incredible Hulk's face appeared. He was in a torn shirt, not a scout's uniform. His green muscles bulged. Inside Usual's head, he could hear his father's laughter as he called Usual a girl. Liking music didn't make him a sissy. It didn't. No matter what his father said.

Usual leaned into the metal trunk again. He would not be ordinary. He'd yelled it at his dad before he left. He meant it then and he meant it now. He pushed with extraordinary effort. The car didn't budge. But it was now vibrating with the coming train. Maybe he had time to take the seat out. What choice did he have? He had to get the baby out some way. Bad luck be damned. It was her baby and surely to God a live crying baby was better than a smashed dead one. All the dead-baby jokes he'd heard at school ran through his mind like a train on some weird track of their own. Maybe this was God's punishment for laughing at them.

What did luck have to do with anything? All that Luck of the Irish crap he'd heard during his father's poker nights was hogwash. Hadn't his father always said people made their own luck? Wasn't that why he'd left to spend the summer here anyway: to make his own luck?

He felt the familiar itch and saw the red splotches appearing on the backs of his hands. Soon he would be covered. Hives or not, he wasn't giving up. He dug his heels in again and prepared to push like he'd never pushed before. He would move this car. That was all there was to it. He took a deep breath and checked the train again. He didn't trust his eyes. He blinked hard and opened wide before he focused. Sure enough. It had switched tracks. Just like that, it was headed east.

Usual heard himself breathing; his throat cramped. The burning under his skin felt like itchy electricity. All he could think now was just how stupid everything was, like a bad dream made worse because nothing made sense.

"I'm Sparrow," the woman called from the clover. She placed a crown on the girl's hair and stood up; she smoothed her skirt and tied her strap on her bare shoulder as she made her way toward Usual. "Pleased to meet you," she said as she extended her hand. When he only stared at it, she turned it over as if examining her fingernails.

"It's like I've told Jayroe, life's too short to worry so much." She waved her hand in the air and let it land on her hip. "I'm heading to Nash-ville." She pronounced it as if it were two separate words. "Just as soon as you get my car fixed, I'll be on my way."

Before he could protest, she was back in the car. "Give 'er another push," she called through the window. This was worse than stupid. He couldn't believe it. His arms and legs felt like silly string only silly string didn't have polka dots. He could barely move. The only thing he wanted to do was slug her and he didn't think he could raise an arm to do even that.

He stepped toward her window and that's when he heard it. The unmistakable release of the emergency brake. The car immediately began to roll on its own. She looked up at him and smiled. They made eye contact for the first time. Then she looked at the road as she steered it off to the side. He watched as she got back out and pushed the lock down through the open window. She twisted at the waist gently, raised her arms and then rubbed her back.

"You probably figured my name's not really Sparrow. That's gonna be my stage name. But I think it suits me better than Mary, don't you?"

Before Usual could say any of the hundred things he was thinking, she lay down in the middle of the road and began to sing. He'd never heard anything like it. He checked the sky for angels, birds, the car radio to see if it was on, anything that might be making the sound, but everything was silent as if someone had hit a secret mute button. Even the roar of the train had disappeared. The only sound he could hear was coming from her. He felt a little dizzy and tried to orient himself by the sun, but the sun would not be still. It kept winking at him. That voice was sure enough hers and she was sure enough right there in front of him, in the middle of County Road 22. It was unbelievable. As the sound swept over him he could feel the words before he heard them. This was obviously a country song, and he hated country music because that's all his dad allowed in their house but her voice was taking the music somewhere beyond the typical clichés, somewhere he, beyond all reason, wanted to follow.

She stopped and sat straight up. "You believe they have Cadillacs in Nashville?"

He didn't know what to believe, so he went for his guitar. He would play if only she would keep singing.

WORK OF ART

by Scott Owens

Nothing new in such incineration,
the potter's shoes were molded through fire,
shaped by merest act of shaping,
baked on in creation's heat,
splattered with unformed parts of pots
and vases, plates and cups, almost
living pieces of earth rubbed
from clay and mud, figures pulled
from open hand, animal head,
body of clay, what matters pinched
between fingertips, pressed
against palm, casting the potter's
pulse and the wheel's pulse into beings
that for the moment, breathe fire.

SPASTIC

by George Singleton

The Calloustown station remains open twenty four hours a day, though no Greyhound or Trailways bus has pulled up for passengers to disembark in fifteen years. The building—plastered-over cement blocks that nearly look stucco, thus exotic among the mobile homes, wooden bungalows, shingle-sided shotgun shacks, and fieldstone salt boxes—holds, still, a linoleum-floored waiting room with chairs shoved in three rows along the walls. There are two restrooms, both with working sinks and toilets, and a glass-fronted booth where someone sold tickets, offered advice, tagged luggage, and so on. A television's mounted on the southwest corner of the waiting room, six inches from touching the ceiling. There's a half-filled gumball machine, the proceeds of which aid small children with birth defects. No one has ever thought to crack open the globe and steal its pennies. An empty cigarette machine with a rust-splattered mirror and rusted silver knobs stands in the corner—$1.75 a pack for Lark, Camel, Lucky Strikes, Pall Mall, Viceroy, Kent, Winston, Marlboro. There's the smell of Juicy Fruit in the air, of plastic, of instant coffee.

The personnel's vanished, the bus line having chosen a different route between Columbia and Savannah, but the electricity's still on. Because there's no community center, YMCA, Lion's Club, rec center,

Moose Club, Jaycees, Kiwanis International, Rotary Club, or Shriners Club in Calloustown, the more community-minded men—the ones who've lived to retirement age, or given up altogether—meet daily at the depot. They have come to realize that their town needs a famous resident in order to attract tourists, which will revive the economy. They have realized that it's better to have a diverse population instead of nearly everyone named either Munson or Harrell. These free-thinkers have concluded that annual festivals—such as their own Sherman Knew Nothing celebration to point out all that the general missed by swerving away between Savannah and Columbia during his march—don't bring in the recognition or revenue. How can, like the old days, a Calloustown child grasp enough knowledge and culture to understand the importance and benefits of fleeing?

Munny Munson says daily, "If our kids fear the outside world, or never comprehend its offerings—good and bad—then those kids will remain here. You think the gene pool's not wet enough to emit a mirage now, just wait another two generations. We got to do something."

On a particularly bleak day, there in the waiting room, one of the other Munsons, or one of a number of men named Harrell, might say, "Low IQs means less personal hygiene. Less hygiene means more contagious diseases. And then everyone dies and people elsewhere might never appreciate William Tecumseh Sherman's apparent myopia." Or one of the men might go off saying, "Lower IQs means less ambition. Less ambition means not taking care of the yard. High grass means field rats. Field rats attract snakes. Bite from a viper on an ambitionless slow-witted person with influenza would be fatal."

For eight hours a day these men nod, clear their throats, blurt out versions of slippery-slope possibilities, all the while watching *The Price is Right*, soap operas, reruns of *I Dream of Jeannie*, *Gilligan's Island*, and *Hogan's Heroes*. They veer from local, state, or national news—"I'm depressed enough, change the channel, I think that one station's doing an *Addams Family* marathon"—and no one ever questions how they could get cable television in a closed-down bus station where no one admits to paying the electric or water bills.

They don't brag about sexual conquests, or reminisce about first times, for each of them has a wife whose brother and cousins stand nearby.

Mack Sloan wipes his soles on the worn rubber Trailways mat out front, turns the knob, and walks into the waiting room. At first he thinks that the men congregated inside laugh at him—as if they judge a man by the overalls he wears and anyone who decides to go out in public wearing fluorescent warm-up pants and a matching windbreaker stands worthless. Then Mack Sloan realizes that the laughter emanates from the television program's laugh track, the volume cranked fully. The men watch *The Honeymooners*.

Mack Sloan nods. Munny Munson stands up and turns the volume knob. He says, "Are you the man from the Guinness Book of Records we been waiting on?"

Mack shakes his head. He says, "I'm turned around a little. Any of you men know where I can find the local high school?"

Flint Harrell stands up and leans his torso backwards awkwardly so that this stranger—the first non-Calloustowner to enter the bus station in fifteen years—can admire Flint's gold-plated belt buckle embossed with SOUTHERN REGION DISCTRICT 4 LEVEL 6 SENIOR DIVISION THIRD PLACE HORSESHOES. Flint says, "If you looking to catch a ride there from here, you're late by 1996. Last bus come through ended up taking people down to those Atlanta Olympics."

Mack Sloan does not feel threatened. He almost laughs. This is perfect—he loves being the first scout in a backwards area, coming out of nowhere like some kind of savior to extract an unknown high school athlete from humble beginnings and promise questionable future monetary outcomes. "No, I got a car out front. Just looking for the high school."

Munny Munson says, "We been waiting on the World Record fellow. Me and Lloyd one time played dominoes for sixty-seven hours straight. That's got to be some kind of record."

And then, as if in a rural AA meeting when the floor opens up for personal testimonial one-upmanship, each man offers his declaration:

"I can lace a pair of logging boots in fourteen seconds."

"I ate four whole barbecued armadillos in twelve minutes."

"I've stared at thirty-two solar eclipses and ain't gone blind yet."

"I trained an ostrich to clean gutters."

Mack Sloan says, "Okay. This sounds like quite a town. Listen, I know it's pretty small here and everyone's probably related to one another. Do any of you know about Brunson Pettigru, the track star? I'm supposed to go clock this fellow and see if he can really do what they say." Sloan pulls a stopwatch from the pocket of his windbreaker, as if to prove his being an authority.

The waiting room regulars quit talking. What did this man mean by "related to one another?" Had word seeped out about the gene pool?

Munny Munson says, ""Track star? No. Never heard of him."

"We don't even have a team anymore, not that I know of," says Flint Harrell.

"Let me see that fancy timepiece," Lloyd says. "I could use one these when I dismantle and reassemble my 1970 Allis Chalmers D270. I believe I got the record unofficially, you know." Then he went into how the world record take-apart-and-put-back-together-a-tractor man might pull in visitors to Calloustown, and then they'd buy hotdogs, and then everyone would gain financially, and then there would be no more threat of pestilence within the failing, bleak, doomed community.

⧓

Mack Sloan, indeed, had not heard of Brunson Pettigru via *Track and Field News*, the Florida Relays, *Runner's World*, or *Parade* magazine. No, a man named Coach Strainer—who taught PE over the internet through the South Carolina Virtual School—boasted of his unknown students on his Facebook page wall: 57% of his students could figure out their BMI. One kid had taken online physical education so seriously that he'd dropped five pounds over the semester, and another could explain all the rules of two different darts games, plus badminton. And then there was Brunson Pettigru of Calloustown, a homeschooled white kid, a six-foot two-inch, 155 pound country boy who had—once he fully understood the cardiovascular system's nuances—dropped his quarter-mile time from fifty-five seconds to forty-six, his half-mile from 2:08 to 1:50.

Sloan understands that, even at a regular high school with traditional teams, coaches exaggerate. He'd scouted, in the past, a boy who heaved a shot-put eighty feet, only to find out the boy's father worked in a machine shop and had shaved weight from the iron sphere. So Mack contacted the S.C. Department of Education, which sent him to the Department of Charter Schools, which sent him to the Department of On-Line Schools, which eventually offered to have Coach Strainer—"one of our finest educators"—contact Mack in Oregon.

"I didn't believe the kid, either," Strainer had said from his office in Myrtle Beach, which doubled as his dining room. "But I seen it with my own two eyes! I got me a friend retired down here from the CIA and he seen it, too, and says they's no way the tape's been sped up doctored."

One of the waiting room men points out the door and says, "School's down there a piece. You won't miss it. They mascot's a ostrich, so they's a big bird right out front of the place. I mean, a sculpture one."

Another man says, "I know who you mean. He ain't no runner, though. He's a spastic."

"We don't want to be famous-known for spastics," says Munny Munson.

≈

Brunson Pettigru's mother homeschooled her only son, for she viewed the public school system in general—and the Calloustown school district in particular—disdainfully. Mrs. Pettigru did not fear that her child might receive secular teaching in regards to science, literature, and religion. To the contrary, she believed a public school filled with children of one denomination only—a school with a population made up almost exclusively of Harrells and Munsons—might corrupt her son into believing in virgin births, no dinosaurs, ribcage wives, and talking bushes. She didn't—unlike 99% of homeschooling parents in South Carolina—choose to direct her son's studies so that they would include daily recitations or sing-alongs of the Pledge of Allegiance, the Lord's Prayer, the Star-Spangled Banner, America the Beautiful, and the Second Amendment of the Constitution. No, Betty Pettigru feared that touched-by-God born-again teachers might chance reprimands and recrimination for "doing what God believes to be right."

"If you want to see yearbook photos of people who did what they

93

thought God wanted them to do, go check out any state's Department of Corrections file of mugshots," she told her son often, as she had told her husband, Finis, before he gave up and died of a heart attack, in the middle of trying to break the world record for smoking cigarettes in a twenty-four hour period.

Mack Sloan drives up to Calloustown High, and sees Brunson wearing vintage gray drawstring sweatpants down at the cinder track that surrounded what might have been a football field. There isn't but one goalpost, for the Calloustown Ostriches won a game due to forfeit three years earlier and the fans in attendance—the team from Forty-Five had been forced to suspend all of its players at the last minute when its appeal was denied by the South Carolina High School Athletic League, in regards to having a number of thirty-year-old players who didn't go to college—stormed the vacant field and, with the use of Harmon Harrell's tractor, knocked over the goalpost and carried it into town. From that point on, when a visiting team scored a touchdown, or wanted to attempt a field goal, the teams had to turn around if indeed they had no goalpost in which to direct a kick.

"You're Brunson?" Mack says when he gets down to the field. "You're Brunson's mom?" he asks the woman who stands there, holding what appears to be wide rubber bands meant for strapping furniture to a flatbed's frame. "I'm Mack Sloan."

Mrs. Pettigru says, "I wouldn't be allowing this to happen if there was homecolleging."

Mack says, "What are those things?" and points at the rubber bands.

He hasn't looked closely at his prospect yet. Brunson wears eyeglasses that appear to be fake, the lenses are so thick. He has them tied to his head with what looks like a bra strap. And in a voice that Mack would later describe as something between a tracheotomist's and a kettle spewing steam, Brunson says, "Because of the cardiovascular limits of the heart vis-à-vis oxygen intake, I tie my forelimbs with these industrial bands before I run so that my most vital organ vis-à-vis the running process does not need to validate anything between my glenohumeral joint and my phalanges."

Mack looks at Brunson. He thinks, *What if aliens come down to the planet and discover this guy? Wouldn't they wonder if they'd never left home?* He says, "All right. You seem to be the kind of guy who might have pre-med in his future."

Mrs. Pettigru, wearing a cotton print dress, says, "My Brunson has always been interested in animals. Does your college have a veterinary program?"

"I like cheetahs," Brunson says. "They're the fastest. If this school had been called the Calloustown Cheetahs, I might have had to fight my mother about allowing me to matriculate. What's your college's mascot?"

"It's a duck. They're not much on land, but they can fly. Some of them can fly."

Mack looks down at Brunson's shoes. The boy wears a pair of regular, flat- and slick-bottomed Keds-brand canvas boatshoes. One of the Pettigrus took a bottle of White Out and marked a Nike swoosh on the sides. Mack says, "Duck."

⤜

Brunson twists and ties his upper biceps with the two rubber bands. He sits down cross-legged on the track. His mother says, "It's important for Brunson to achieve the correct amount of tingling in his arms before he runs a lap."

Mack Sloan thinks, *There's no way I'll ever recommend offering this kid a scholarship.* He thinks, *People think members of our track team are freaks already?—get a load of this new guy!* He thinks, *Hell, I'm here—I might as well see what happens.* He thinks, *Cardiovascular vis-à-vis cheetah glenohumeral joint and my phalanges veterinary school vital organ homecolleging.*

"A fun thing to do is have me run a quarter-mile without the additional garments, and then compare and contrast what happens once my heart no longer has to pump blood to needless expanses," Brunson says.

"Okay," Mack says. He'd dealt with runners who insisted on smoking pot the night before a race, runners who drank six beers the night before a race, runners who had to fuck two different women before a race, then another one a couple hours before the starting gun. Mack had dealt with runners—world class runners—who insisted on eating sushi, or Vienna sausages, or Fig Newtons. He'd had runners who had to watch *Godfather III* the night before a big race, and others who insisted that virgins recite

95

the poems of Gerard Manley Hopkins.

But not this.

"You about ready?" Mack says.

Betty Pettigru says, "I'm going to take my spot in the stands. I always sit in the stands. When I'm in the stands, my son's never lost a race."

"Wait a minute," Mack says. "So you're on the track team here?"

"I've never been in an actual race," Brunson says. "Do you think that might make a difference? I mean, psychologically, it might make me run either faster or slower."

While I'm down this way, Mack Sloan thinks, *I might as well go down to Myrtle Beach and kill that Coach Strainer dude.*

"Uh-oh," Brunson says. He stands up, and half-lifts one arm toward the parking lot. "Somebody's here."

Mack turns around to see every man whom he'd met at the bus depot. They walk down the embankment. One of them says, "We just thought we'd come on down here and see if we got us a savior."

Mack pulls the stopwatch out of his pocket. He says, "I didn't even think to ask—are you sure this is a quarter-mile track? It looks like a quarter-mile, but are you sure?"

"It's 440 yards," Brunson says. "I've circled it ten times with the Lufkin MW18TP Measuring Wheel, and it came out to 13,200 feet. And then I divided that by three, which comes out to 4,400 yards, and then divided that by ten, which comes out to 440 yards. I thought about doing a hundred laps, just to make sure, but it was getting dark and I still had to write a term paper for my mother comparing and contrasting the Suez Canal with the Panama Canal. A cheetah can swim across both of them, by the way. A cheetah's not the fastest swimmer, but it can swim."

"I'm ready!" Betty Pettigru yells from the wooden bleachers.

The bus depot men arrive trackside. One of them says, "I don't know."

Mack Sloan says to Brunson, "You don't need any blocks or any-thing? Don't you think you better stretch, or warm up a little? You might want to take off your sweats, too."

Munny Munson says, "I still believe we got a better shot at making Calloustown famous if we become home to a serial killer, as opposed to a spastic." He says, "Hell, Betty Pettigru's ex-husband had the right idea, up until he smoked himself to death."

"I'd like to fuck her," one of the Harrells says. "She ain't nobody's sister."

Brunson says, "I've heard about those block things. Do you think they'll really help?"

He pulls off his sweatpants to reveal what may or may not be an old pair of his mother's hot pants from the 1970s. When he toes the line, his arms swing half-useless.

⤜

"Go!" Mack Sloan says. He's performed this task so many times he can't remember. He has timed prospective athletes in thirty states. He's gone down to Central America and found sprinters, South America for middle distance runners, and Africa for long-distance runners.

Brunson takes off. His mother bellows, "Catch that big cat, honey, catch that big cat!" and makes some odd noises in between, like long, extended *Ummms* that might point toward a nervous tic, or Tourette's. Mack Sloan keeps his eyes on his prospect, but the Munson and Harrell men stare up toward the stands. Betty Pettigru's mid-sentence, guttural noises—by the time Brunson hits the 220 mark—now sound as if they're caused by orgasm.

"Jesus Christ," Mack says. "Twenty two seconds flat." He yells out to Brunson, "Keep it coming, my man. Push through it. Keep your form!"

Brunson takes the back straightaway and—there was no way for Mack Sloan to explain this later to his colleagues—his arms go haywire. He keeps running well, and stays in his lane, but his arms, out of blood flow, look similar to those twenty-five-foot ripstop nylon sky tubes normally used for advertising purposes in the parking lots of car dealerships, mattress warehouses, and buffet-style restaurants managed by the criminally insane.

Is the kid dancing? Mack thinks. Is he fighting demons that no one but his mother—still ululating in the stands—can see?

He clicks the stopwatch when Brunson hits the finish line, slows down to a jog, and continues forward, untying the rubber bands from his arms. Forty-six flat, sure enough, just like Virtual Coach Strainer declared. Mack Sloan looks up in the bleachers and notices how Betty Pettigru sits with her legs splayed open. He looks at the bus depot men and says, "I've never seen anything like this in all my years. I've been coaching since I was out of college. This is the damnedest place I've ever seen. Is this one of those trick TV shows? Is someone playing a trick on me, and I'm being filmed covertly?"

Munny Munson says, "I bet I know why old Finis's heart give out, and it didn't have nothing to do with smoking 144 cigarettes in a row the way he done. Hot damn, that woman's a regular vixen."

"She appears to love her son, you got that right," says Mack Sloan. He calls Brunson back to him, but keeps looking up in the stands. Betty Pettigru has pulled her hair up in some kind of topknot. "Listen, don't you men have something to do with yourselves? I'm working here."

Mack jogs down the track. He says, "Good God, man, you can flat-out fly. But I don't know about those rubber bands around your arms. I'm not so sure they'd let you run like that in a race, what with the possibility of injuring other runners. Especially in the 800."

Brunson says, "What about if I go ahead and cut off my arms? Is that what you want? I'm not going to cut off my arms just to please you."

Mrs. Pettigru comes down from the bleachers and says, "Brunson. Don't start, Brunson."

"I'm sorry."

"Brunson has some anger issues," Mrs. Pettigru says. "That might be an overstatement. He has some issues with patience."

"Can I see you run without those strange rubber bands?" Mack asks.

Betty Pettigru stands close to Mack. *Is she flirting with me?* he wonders. *Is this her way of seeing her son get a scholarship?*

"Do you have no imagination?" Brunson blurts out. "You saw me run once. Now imagine me running again, without the rubber bands that enhance my cardiovascular capabilities."

Mrs. Pettigru says, "Brunson," again, this time drawling out his name, in a higher pitch.

"Is there any place we can sit down and talk?" Mack asks. He wonders if the rubber bands affected the oxygen supply to Brunson's head, thus causing the sudden evident fury.

"I'm sorry," Brunson says. "I'm sorry, sorry, sorry," he says, and takes off running around the track, then over a fence and into the woods.

Betty Pettigru looks at her wristwatch. She says, "I'm about ready for a martini. What about you, Coach?"

≈

There's no one inside Worm's Bar and Grill. There's no bartender, either. Betty Pettigru walks behind the counter, pulls a fifth of Absolut off the shelf, and pours four shots into a metal shaker, throws in some ice, swirls it around, and pours two glasses to the brim. "I like mine dry," she says. "You want an olive in yours? Worm doesn't believe in cocktail onions."

"Yeah, I'll take a couple olives," Mack says. He had followed Betty on the one mile drive between the high school and downtown Callous-town, and noticed that she drank something from a Thermos along the way.

Betty Pettigru slides a jar of Thrifty Maid-brand green olives down the counter. She says, "This should answer any questions about why I didn't move away when Brunson's daddy died. Not many places around will let you walk in and drink on the honor system."

"Will he be all right?" Mack asks. "I'm worried about him."

"No, he's probably going to stay dead. We had him cremated, so even the most advanced advances in science won't bring him back." She walks around the counter and sits down on a stool beside Mack.

She puts her hand on his shoulder.

"I'm talking about your son. Is he going to be all right, that's what I meant."

"He's fine. He has a lot of things on his mind. He took the SAT and scored perfect on the math but only made a 740 on the verbal. He's taking the thing again."

Mack drinks and says, "This is like straight vodka."

"I don't know what I'm going to do when he leaves the nest. Listen. Do you think the university would want a student who scored a perfect SAT and can run that fast? I'm willing to bet that just about every college would want such a student."

Mack thinks, *Is that lipstick, or are her lips really that red?* He thinks, *I need to make some promises I can't keep.* "I'm thinking Brunson wouldn't have a problem getting a full ride."

"And what about me?" Betty says. She scoots over closer. "I hear tell of some colleges hiring on parents, you know, to work at the college. Coach. Work as a secretary. Me, I could fit right in teaching in the Education department, seeing as I'm batting nearly perfect with my past students."

Mack Sloan nods and laughs. He says, "I don't know of any bars that'll let you go in there and drink on the honor system, though."

She puts her hand on his left thigh. Mack thinks, *No, no, no, no, no.* He says, "It's only track and field, Ms. Pettigru. It's not like football or basketball."

"I like to do this in alphabetical order," she says, getting up from the barstool. "Absolut done, and Grey Goose next." She looks at the bottles lined up. "Worm got some Ketel One! That'll be a good segue before I get on to that cheap shit Seagram's and Smirnoff, before heading out to the," she picks up a bottle and raises her eyebrows to Mack, "Three Olives."

"You're going to have to go that route alone, I'm afraid," Mack says. "I got to get down the road and check out a two-miler from somewhere," he lies, though in fact he's scheduled to talk to a distance runner from Georgia tomorrow.

The phone rings. Betty shrugs and picks it up. She says, "Hello?" instead of "Worm's Bar and Grill." Mack stands up and thinks about going to his car and driving away. Betty says into the receiver, "I'm not doing anything wrong. You can come on over here and see for yourself," and then the door opens, Brunson walks in with a cell phone to his head, and both he and his mother hang up.

Brunson says, "I told you I could rig this cell phone to get good reception, even here where we don't get reception." He says to Mack Sloan, "I've been reconsidering."

His mother walks back carrying the bottles of Grey Goose and Ketel One. She says, "I'm about to get you a football scholarship, too, boy."

Brunson says, "Can I have a beer, Mom?" He says, "After I drink some olive juice to replace the salt I lost running, can I have a beer?"

Betty reaches over the bar and slides back the cooler top. She reaches in and gets a can of PBR. To Mack Sloan she says, "I'm not a bad mother. Or a whore."

≈

Worm walks in through the back door. He says, "Well, well, well, I heard we had us a big-shot stranger in town. Hey, Betty Pettigru." He keeps his eyes locked on Mack. "Hey, Brunson. You got your ID for that beer?"

Brunson says, "I forgot it again."

"Bring it on in next time," Worm says. He wears a sleeveless white dress shirt, blue jeans with holes in the knees. He sports a tattoo on each arm—a speed bag on his left, and a heavy bag on the right. To Mack he says, "Just come back from the depot. You're the talk of Calloustown." Worm sticks out his hand to shake, which Mack does. "Next to some old boy from the Guinness World Record book showing up, I guess you're about all that and a roll of duct tape, ain't you?"

Mack doesn't know what he means. He says, "Are you a boxer, or ex-boxer?" and points to the tattoos. Betty Pettigru leads her son over to the jukebox. They stare at its buttons and choices as if it were a time machine. "That's the way we are here in Calloustown," Worm says. "We try to make things easier for everything. Back in the day, my great-great-grandmother went out to what wasn't I-95 and tried to lead General Sherman back to Calloustown so he could burn it. Least that's the story. Anyway, back when I was in junior high school I got bullied a bunch, seeing as I'm so skinny and got called Worm, so later on—maybe in the tenth grade—I went over the state line and got these tattoos so my enemies would have a target to punch, you know."

Betty and Brunson return to the stools. Worm goes around the other side, to work as the bartender. Brunson says, "I guess I could try out as something like a kick returner. If you confess that my mom's not a whore, then I'll be willing to try out as a kick returner."

Mack tries to think if he actually called Betty a whore. Worm slides another double shot of cold vodka his way. He says, "Because of all that

101

reading you do, Brunson, I'm sure you've come across how constant—heck, even infrequent—constriction of limbs can result in nerve damage. Next thing you know you got gangrene and have to have the limb amputated."

What else can I say? Mack thinks. He thinks, *I need to get out of here before anyone starts pulling out pistols.* Not that he was a big reader, but he'd come across stories about people in the South.

Brunson drinks his beer like a professional. He says, "I don't care. What would it matter? If getting my arms cut off in the future is the only way I can get out of Calloustown, so be it."

"You don't mean that," his mother says.

"Come over here and hit me in the arm," says Worm. He tenses his muscles. "What you need, boy, is a tattoo like mine. That's what's made it worthwhile for me to stay."

"When's the last time the cigarette man came by here, Worm? I want me a pack of cigarettes, but I don't want any of those you got in there stale. As I recall, Finis bought his last cigarettes from that machine," Betty says. She pulls the hem of her dress right on up to her eyes and wipes them, showing off a pair of panties that weren't bought anywhere in South Carolina, Mack thinks—"Shake, Rattle, and Roll" printed in red lettering across the front. She says, "I'm sorry. I don't even think Brunson knows this, but it's our anniversary." To Mack she says, "How about you giving me an anniversary present."

Brunson hits the floor. He either wants attention, or undergoes a full-scale seizure. Mack says, "I have a carton of cigarettes out in the car. Let me go get you a couple packs."

"Menthol?" Betty says.

"Yeah. Let me go get them right now for you. Is Brunson okay?" he asks as he opens the door.

Mack Sloan starts up the car and takes off. He needs to U-turn at some point, but he wants out of there. *There's something bad in the water here,* he thinks. He thinks, *I will go back home and say that the Virtual High School P.E. teacher didn't know what he's talking about.* He turns on the radio and hits Search, only to find nothing, then switches over to AM stations, hits Search, and still finds nothing. He thinks, *A forty-six second quarter-miler with a near-perfect SAT. When will I ever come across another one of those?* Mack flips open his cell phone and gets no signal.

When he approaches the bus depot he notices that a number of handwritten signs now dot the roadside: Told You So. Don't Come Back Unless You Mean It. Sherman Sucked, Too.

What can he do but turn around? What can he do but try not to think ahead to the future, when he's sitting around his house at night, awaiting a knock at the door, knowing that someone wants to come in and talk about his or her problems in regards to homesickness, or nerves? The radio catches a station. A man gives the weather report and says that the drought has been modified from extreme to exceptional. He reminds listeners to put water out for animals, and notes that not all foaming-mouthed dogs have contracted rabies.

≈ SMASH & GRAB ≈
by Michael Knight

At the last house on the left, the one with no security system sign staked on the lawn, no dog in the backyard, Cashdollar elbowed out a pane of glass in the kitchen door and reached through to unlock it from the inside. Though he was 99% certain that the house was empty—he'd watched the owners leave himself—he paused a moment just across the threshold, listened carefully, heard nothing. Satisfied, he padded through an archway into the dining room where he found a chest of silverware and emptied its contents into the pillowcase he'd brought. He was headed down the hall, looking for the master bedroom, hoping that, in the rush to make some New Year's Eve soiree, the lady of the house had left her jewelry in plain sight, when he saw a flash of white and his head was snapped back on his neck, the bones in his face suddenly aflame. He wobbled, dropped to his knees. Then a girlish grunt and another burst of pain and all he knew was darkness.

≈

He came to with his wrists and ankles bound with duct tape to the arms and legs of a ladder-back chair. His cheeks throbbed. His nose felt huge with ache. Opposite him, in an identical chair, a teenage girl was blowing lightly on the fingers of her left hand. There was a porcelain toilet tank lid, flecked with blood, across her lap. On it was arrayed a pair of cuticle scissors, a bottle of clear polish, cotton balls and a nail file. The girl glanced up at him now and he would have sworn she was pleased to find him awake.

"How's your face?" she said.

She was long-limbed, lean but not skinny, wearing a T-shirt with the words *Saint Bridget's Volleyball* across the front in pastel plaids. Her hair was pulled into pigtails. She wore flannel boxers and pink wool socks.

"It hurts like hell." His nostrils were plugged with blood, his voice buzzing like bad wiring in his head.

The girl did a sympathetic wince.

"I thought no one was home," he said.

"I guess you cased the house?" she said. "Is that the word—cased?"

Cashdollar nodded and she gave him a look, like she was sorry for spoiling his plans.

"I'm at boarding school. I just flew in this afternoon."

"I didn't see a light," he said.

"I keep foil over the windows," she said. "I need total darkness when I sleep. There's weather stripping under the door and everything."

"Have you called the police?"

"Right after I knocked you out. You scared me so bad I practically just shouted my address into the phone and hung up." She giggled a little at herself. "I was afraid you'd wake up and kill me. That's why the tape. I'll call again if they aren't here soon." This last she delivered as if she regretted having to make him wait. She waggled her fingers at him. "I was on my left pinky when I heard the window break."

Cashdollar estimated at least ten minutes for the girl to drag him down the hall and truss him up, which meant that the police would be arriving momentarily. He had robbed houses in seven states, had surprised his share of homeowners, but he'd never once had a run-in with the law. He was too fast on his feet for that, strictly smash and grab, never got greedy, never resorted to violence. Neither, however, had a teenage girl ever bashed him unconscious with a toilet lid and duct-taped him to a chair.

"This boarding school," he said. "They don't send you home for

Christmas."

"I do Christmas with my Mom," she said.

Cashdollar waited a moment for her to elaborate but she was quiet and he wondered if he hadn't hit on the beginnings of an angle here, wondered if he had time enough to work it. When it was clear that she wasn't going to continue, he prompted her.

"Divorce is hard," he said.

The girl shrugged. "Everybody's divorced."

"So the woman I saw before…" He let the words trail off into a question.

"My father's girlfriend," she said. "One of." She rolled her eyes. "My dad—last of the big time swingers."

"Do you like her?" he said. "Is she nice?"

"I hardly know her. She's a nurse. She works for him." She waved a hand before her face as if swiping at an insect. "I think it's tacky if you want to know the truth."

They were in the dining room, though Cashdollar hadn't bothered to take it in when he was loading up the silverware. He saw crown molding. He saw paintings on the walls, dogs and dead birds done in oils, expensive but without resale value. This was a doctor's house, he thought. It made him angry that he'd misread the presence of the woman, angrier even than the fact that he'd let himself get caught. He was thirty-six years old. That seemed to him just then like a long time to be alive.

"I'm surprised you don't have a date," he said. "Pretty girl like you home alone on New Year's Eve."

He had his doubts about flattery—the girl seemed too sharp for that—but she took his remark in stride.

"Like I said, I just got in today and I'm away at school most of the year. Plus, I spend more time with my mother in California than my father so I don't really know anybody here."

"What's your name?" he said.

The girl hesitated. "I'm not sure I should tell you that."

"I just figured if you told me your name and I told you mine then you'd know somebody here."

"I don't think so," she said.

Cashdollar closed his eyes. He was glad that he wasn't wearing some kind of burglar costume, the black sweatsuit, the ski mask. He felt less obvious in street clothes. Tonight, he'd chosen a hunter green coat, a navy turtleneck, khaki pants and boat shoes. He didn't bother wearing gloves. He wasn't so scary looking this way, he thought, and when he asked the question that was on his mind, it might seem like one regular person asking a favor of another.

"Listen, I'm just going to come right out and say this, okay? I'm wondering what are the chances you'd consider letting me go?" The girl opened her mouth but Cashdollar pressed ahead before she could refuse and she settled back into her chair to let him finish. "Because the police will be here soon and I don't want to go to prison and I promise, if you let me, I'll leave the way I came in and vanish from your life forever."

The girl was quiet for a moment, her face patient and composed, as if waiting to be sure he'd said his piece. He could hear the refrigerator humming in the kitchen. A moth plinked against the chandelier over their heads. He wondered if it hadn't slipped in through the broken pane. The girl capped the bottle of nail polish, lifted the toilet lid from her lap without disturbing the contents and set it on the floor beside her chair.

"I'm sorry," she said. "I really am, but you did break into the house and you put my father's silverware in your pillowcase and I'm sure you would have taken other things if I hadn't hit you on the head. If you want, I'll tell the police that you've been very nice, but I don't think it's right for me to let you go."

In spite—or because of—her genial demeanor, Cashdollar was beginning to feel like his heart was on the blink; it felt as thick and rubbery as a hot water bottle in his chest. He held his breath and strained against his bonds, hard enough to hop his chair, once, twice, but the tape held fast. He sat there, panting.

The girl said, "Let me ask you something. Let's say I was asleep or watching TV or whatever and I didn't hear the window break. Let's say you saw me first—what would you have done?"

He didn't have to think about his reply.

"I would have turned around and left the house. I've never hurt anyone in my whole life."

The girl stared at him for a long moment then dropped her eyes, fanned her fingers, studied her handiwork. She didn't look altogether pleased. To the backs of her hands she said, "I believe you."

As if to punctuate her sentence, the doorbell rang, followed by four sharp knocks, announcing the arrival of the police.

~

While he waited, Cashdollar thought about prison. The possibility of incarceration loomed forever on the periphery of his life but he'd never allowed himself to waste a lot of time considering the specifics. He told himself that at least he wasn't leaving anyone behind, wasn't ruining anyone else's life, though even as he filled his head with reassurances, he understood that they were false and his pulse was roaring in his ears, his lungs constricting. He remembered this one break-in down in Pensacola when some sound he made—a rusty hinge? a creaking floorboard?— startled the owner of the house from sleep. The bedroom was dark and the man couldn't see Cashdollar standing at the door. "Violet?" he said. "Is that you, Vi?" There was such sadness, such longing in his voice that Cashdollar knew Violet was never coming back. He pitied the man, of course, but at the same time, he felt as if he was watching him through a window, felt outside the world looking in rather than in the middle of things with the world pressing down around him. The man rolled over, mumbled his way back to sleep, and Cashdollar crept out of the house feeling sorry for himself. He hadn't thought about that man in years. Now he could hear voices in the next room but he couldn't make out what they were saying. It struck him that they were taking too long and he wondered if this wasn't what people meant when they described time bogging down at desperate moments.

Then the girl rounded the corner into the dining room trailing a pair of uniformed police officers, the first a white guy, straight out of central casting, big and pudgy, his tunic crumpled into his slacks, his belt slung low under his belly, the second, a black woman, small with broad shoulders, her hair twisted into braids under her cap. "My friend—" The girl paused, shot a significant look at Cashdollar. —"Patrick, surprised him in the dining room and the burglar hit him with the toilet thingy and taped him up. Patrick, these are Officers Hildebran and Pruitt." She tipped her head right, then left to indicate the man and the woman respectively.

Officer Pruitt circled around behind Cashdollar's chair.

"What was the burglar doing with a toilet lid?"

"That's a mystery," the girl said.

"Why haven't you cut him loose?"

"We didn't know what to do for sure," the girl said. "He didn't seem to be hurt too bad and we didn't want to disturb the crime scene. On TV, they always make a big deal out of leaving everything just so."

"I see," said Officer Pruitt, exactly as if she didn't see at all. "And you did your nails to pass the time?" She pointed at the manicure paraphernalia.

The girl made a goofy, self-deprecating face, all eyebrows and lips, and twirled her finger in the air beside her ear.

Officer Hildebran wandered over to the window. Without facing the room, he said, "I'll be completely honest with you, Miss Schnell—"

"Daphne," the girl said, and Cashdollar had the sense that her interjection was meant for him.

Officer Hildebran turned, smiled. "I'll be honest, Daphne, we sometimes recover some of the stolen property but—"

"He didn't take anything," the girl said.

Officer Hildebran raised his eyebrows. "No?"

"He must have panicked," Daphne said.

Cashdollar wondered what had become of his pillowcase, figured it was still in the hall where the girl had ambushed him, hoped the police didn't decide to poke around back there. Officer Pruitt crouched at his knees to take a closer look at the duct tape.

"You all right?" she said.

He nodded, cleared his throat.

"Where'd the tape come from?"

"I don't know," he said. "I was out cold."

"Regardless," Officer Hildebran was saying to Daphne, "unless there's a reliable eyewitness—"

Officer Pruitt sighed. "There is an eyewitness." She raised her eyes, regarded Cashdollar's battered face.

"Oh," Officer Hildebran said. "Right. You think you could pick him out of a line-up?"

"It all happened pretty fast," Cashdollar said.

And so it went, as strange and vivid as a fever dream, their questions, his answers, their questions, Daphne's answers—he supposed that she was not the kind of girl likely to arouse suspicion, not the kind of girl people were inclined to disbelieve—until the police were satisfied, more or less. They seemed placated by the fact that Cashdollar's injuries weren't severe and that nothing had actually been stolen. Officer Pruitt cut the tape with a utility knife and Cashdollar walked them to the door like he was welcome in this house. He invented contact information, assured them that he'd be down in the morning to look at mugshots. He didn't know what had changed Daphne's mind and, watching the police make their way down the sidewalk and out of his life, he didn't care. He shut the door and said, "Is Daphne your real name?" He was just turning to face her when she clubbed him with the toilet lid again.

～

Once more, Cashdollar woke in the ladder-back chair, wrists and ankles bound, but this time Daphne was seated cross-legged on the floor, leaned back, her weight on her hands. He saw her as if through a haze, as if looking through a smeary lens, noticed her long neck, the smooth skin on the insides of her thighs.

"Yes," Daphne said.

"What?"

"Yes, my name is Daphne."

"Oh," he said.

His skull felt full of sand.

"I'm sorry for conking you again," she said. "I don't know what happened. I mean, it was such a snap decision to lie to the police and then that woman cut the tape and I realized I don't know the first thing about you and I freaked." She clipped her thumbnail between her teeth. "What's your name?" she said.

Cashdollar felt as if he was being lowered back into himself from a great height, gradually remembering how it was to live in his body. Before he was fully aware of what he was saying, he'd given her an honest answer.

Daphne laughed. "I wasn't expecting that. I didn't think anybody named anybody Leonard anymore."

"I'm much older than you."

"You're not so old. What are you, forty?"

"Thirty-six."

Daphne said, "Oops."

"I think I have a concussion," Cashdollar said.

Daphne wrinkled her nose apologetically and pushed to her feet and brushed her hands together. "Be right back," she said. She ducked into the kitchen, returned with a highball glass, which she held under his chin. He smelled scotch, let her bring it to his mouth. It tasted expensive.

"Better?" Daphne said.

Cashdollar didn't answer. He'd been inclined to feel grateful but hadn't the vaguest idea where this was going now. She sat on the floor and he watched her sip from the glass. She made a retching face, shuddered, regrouped.

"At school one time, I drank two entire bottles of Robitussin cough syrup. I hallucinated that my Klimt poster was coming to life. It was very sexual. My roommate called the paramedics."

"Is that right?" Cashdollar said.

"My father was in Aruba when it happened," she said. "He was with an AMA rep named Farina Hoyle. I mean, what kind of a name is Farina Hoyle? He left her there and flew all the way back to make sure I was all right."

"That's nice, I guess," Cashdollar said.

Daphne nodded and smiled, half-sly, half-something else. Cashdollar couldn't put his finger on what he was seeing in her face. "It isn't true," she said. "Farina Hoyle's true. Aruba's true."

"What are you going to do with me?" Cashdollar said.

Daphne peered into the glass.

"I don't know," she said.

They were quiet for a minute. Daphne swirled the whisky. Cashdollar's back itched and he rubbed it on the chair. When Daphne saw what he was doing, she moved behind the chair to scratch it for him and he tipped forward to give her better access. Her touch raised goosebumps, made his skin jump like horseflesh.

"Are you married?" she said.

He told her, "No."

"Divorced?"

He shook his head. Her hand went still between his shoulder blades. He heard her teeth click on the glass.

"You poor thing," she said. "Haven't you ever been in love?"

"I think you should cut me loose," Cashdollar said.

Daphne came around the chair and sat on his knee, draped her arm over his shoulder.

"How often do you do this? Rob houses, I mean."

"I do it when I need the money," he said.

"When was the last time?" Her face was close enough that he could smell the liquor on her breath.

"A while ago," he said. "Could I have another sip of that?" She helped him with the glass. He felt the scotch behind his eyes. The truth was he'd done an apartment house just last week, waited at the door for somebody to buzz him up, then broke the locks on the places where no one was home. Just now, however, he didn't see the percentage in the truth. He said, "I only ever do rich people and I give half my take to Jerry's Kids."

Daphne socked him in the chest.

"Ha, ha," she said.

"Isn't that what you want to hear?" he said. "Right? You're looking for a reason to let me go?"

"I don't know," she said.

He shrugged. "Who's to say it isn't true?"

"Jerry's Kids," she said.

She was smiling and he smiled back. He couldn't help liking this girl. He liked that she was smart and that she wasn't too afraid of him. He liked that she had the guts to bullshit the police.

"Ha, ha," he said.

Daphne knocked back the last of the scotch, then skated her socks over the hardwood floor, headed for the window.

"Do you have a car?" she said, parting the curtains. "I don't see a car."

"I'm around the block," he said.

"What do you drive?"

"Honda Civic."

Daphne raised her eyebrows.

"It's inconspicuous," he said.

She skated back over to his chair and slipped her hand into his pocket and rooted for his keys. Cashdollar flinched. There were only two keys on the ring, his car and his apartment. For some reason, this embarrassed him.

"It really is a Honda," Daphne said.

⁓

There was a grandfather clock in the corner but it had died at half past eight who knew how long ago and his watch was out of sight beneath the duct tape and Cashdollar was beginning to worry about the time. He guessed Daphne had been gone for twenty minutes, figured he was safe until after midnight, figured her father and his lady friend would at least ring in the New Year before calling it a night. He put the hour around eleven but he couldn't be sure and for all he knew, Daphne was out there joyriding in his car and you couldn't tell what might happen at a party on New Year's Eve. Somebody might get angry. Somebody might have too much to drink. Somebody might be so crushed with love they can't wait another minute to get home. He went on thinking like this until he heard what sounded like a garage door rumbling open and his mind went blank and he narrowed the whole of his perception to his ears. For a minute, he heard nothing—he wasn't going to mistake silence for safety a second time—then a door opened in the kitchen and Daphne breezed into the room.

"Took me a while to find your car," she said.

She had changed clothes for her foray into the world. Now, she was wearing an electric blue parka with fur inside the hood and white leggings and knee-high alpine boots.

"What time is it?" he said.

But she passed through without stopping, disappeared into the next room.

"You need to let me go," he said.

When she reappeared, she was carrying a stereo speaker, her back arched under its weight. He watched her into the kitchen. She returned a minute later, empty-handed, breathing hard.

"I should've started small," she said.

He looked at her. "I don't understand."

"It's a good thing you've got a hatchback."

For the next half hour, she shuttled between the house and the garage, bearing valuables each trip, first the rest of the stereo, then the TV and the Blu-ray, then his pillowcase of silverware, then an armload of expensive-looking suits and on and on until Cashdollar was certain that his car would hold no more. Still she kept it up. Barbells, golf clubs, a calfskin luggage set. A pair of antique pistols. A dusty classical guitar. A baseball signed by someone dead and famous. With each passing minute, Cashdollar could feel his stomach tightening and it was all he could do to keep his mouth shut but he had the sense that he should leave her be, that this didn't have anything to do with him. He pictured his little Honda bulging with the accumulated property of another man's life, flashed to his apartment in his mind, unmade bed, lawn chairs in the living room, coffee mug in the sink. He made a point of never holding on to anything anybody else might want to steal. There was not a single thing in his apartment that it would hurt to lose, nothing he couldn't live without. Daphne swung back into the room, looking frazzled, her face glazed with perspiration.

"There." She huffed at a wisp of hair that had fallen across her eyes.

"You're crazy," Cashdollar said.

Daphne dismissed him with a wave.

"You're out of touch," she said. "I'm your average sophomore."

"What'll you tell the cops?"

"I like Stockholm Syndrome but I think they're more likely to believe you made me lie under threat of death." She took the parka off, draped it on a chair, lifted the hem of her sweatshirt to wipe her face, exposing her belly, the curve of her ribs, pressed it first against her right eye, then her left as if dabbing tears.

"I'll get the scissors," Daphne said.

She went out again, came back again. The tape fell away like something dead. Cashdollar rubbed his wrists a second, pushed to his feet and they stood there looking at each other. Her eyes, he decided, were the color of a jade pendant he had stolen years ago. That pendant pawned for $700.00. It flicked through his mind that he should kiss her and that she would let him but he restrained himself. He had no business kissing teenage girls. Then, as if she could read his thoughts, Daphne slapped him across the face. Cashdollar palmed his cheek, blinked the sting away, watched her doing a girlish bob and weave, her thumbs tucked inside her fists.

"Let me have it," she said.

"Quit," he said.

"Wimp," she said. "I dropped you twice."

"I'm gone," he said.

Right then, she poked him in the nose. It wouldn't have hurt so much if she hadn't already hit him with the toilet lid but as it was, his eyes watered up, his vision filled with tiny sparkles. Without thinking, he balled his hand and punched her in the mouth, not too hard, a reflex, just enough to sit her down, but right away he felt sick at what he'd done. He held his palms out, like he was trying to stop traffic.

"I didn't mean that," he said. "That was an accident. I've never hit a girl. I've never hurt anyone in my life."

Daphne touched her bottom lip, smudging her fingertip with blood.

"This will break his heart," she said.

She smiled at Cashdollar and he could see blood in the spaces between her teeth. The sight of her dizzied him with sadness. He thought how closely linked were love and pain. Daphne extended a hand, limp-wristed, ladylike. Her nails were perfect.

"Now tape me to the chair," she said.

⊸ BURNING BLUE ⊷

by Jennifer Paddock

One of my favorite things I heard at the Shoe Burnin'—and I'm not sure who said it—was this: "Somebody's shoes is burning blue." Suzanne Hudson told me that Milton Brown—a movie producing, hit-songwriting guy who helped launch Jimmy Buffett's career—said it and that a blue flame signifies the purest spirit.

When I think of pure spirits, I think of my father, a kind man who did one unkind thing by killing himself.

There was a time when I was embarrassed to tell anyone how my father died. Embarrassed for me and for the people I told when they'd have to react. I clung to anyone whose father had died. I fell in love with a boy largely because of this connection. I wrote about this in my novel, *A Secret Word*. Here is how truth translated to fiction:

On my first date with Evan, we talked about our fathers. I told him the truth, that my father had killed himself over his failing law practice. How he'd done it in a warehouse early in the morning with a shotgun. How he'd left a letter on the kitchen table to my mother, and how I hoped to find, in my mailbox in New York, every day for weeks, a letter to me. I had been telling people that he died of a heart attack while playing golf.

Evan told me about how his father died slowly of a brain tumor when Evan was twelve. How Evan would go to visit him in a hospital, and his father would be in a

wheelchair drooling, obese from the tumor. "I was still a kid, you know," Evan said.
"And this was my father. And I was embarrassed."

One thing I hope my contribution does is take away some of the
stigma that surrounds suicide.

AND WHEN I SHOULD FEEL SOMETHING
excerpted from *A Secret Word*

April 1996
Chandler

I call my parents to see how everything is in Arkansas. It's the first
nice spring day in New York, and I want to tell my father about jogging
through Central Park. My mother answers the phone and sounds different, distracted, and says she'll call me back. I read the paper, watch television, and when my mother calls, she says my father has killed himself.

My mom has arranged for a friend's son to take me to the airport.
He lives in New Brunswick, New Jersey, and will be here in an hour. He
will buy my ticket, and my mother will reimburse his father.

I'm not ready when he buzzes my apartment, but I let him up anyway
and try to finish packing before he gets upstairs. I open the door and
see a guy and girl, about my age, twenty-four, and hold my hand out to
the guy, trying to be polite, and say, "I'm Chandler." He shakes my hand
and says his name, then he introduces his girlfriend, but I don't listen. I
apologize for not being ready. They ask if they can help me pack, but I
say, "No. Thank you. I'll just be a minute."

They watch me, and they look around. They look at my bedroom, at
my bookshelf, at the small kitchen that is part of the living room.

Driving to the airport, there is traffic, and I wish he had taken the
tunnel. We don't talk much, except about the traffic. I wish I were in a
cab.

At the American Airlines counter, he buys my ticket home. "Twelve
hundred dollars to Fort Smith, Arkansas," he says, handing it to me.
"I'm glad Dad's the one who's buying it." His girlfriend gives him a look,
and I say, "Thank you. I really appreciate everything." I don't want to be
indebted to him, but I am. I give him and his girlfriend an awkward hug

goodbye.

Waiting in line to board the plane, a woman asks me what time it is. I pause too long. The woman says, "My watch stopped." I tell her two-thirty. Once seated, I cry. I don't want to make a scene. I don't want anyone to ask me what's wrong. I put my book in the pocket of the seat in front of me, then I look for it, thinking I put it in my bag. My face is hot and streaked with tears.

At home, people turn and look at me and whisper. My mother doesn't seem right. She's acting light-headed, in a fluttering way, like she's at a party. "Oh, Chandler," she says when she sees me.

Flowers are everywhere, and my mother tells me that there are some for me by the fireplace. I guess Sarah has heard the news. She sent a huge, flashy bouquet, gladiolas and Easter lilies.

A childhood friend of mine is here, my first boyfriend in the sixth grade, and I motion for him to follow me upstairs. "I'm glad you're here," I tell him.

He says, "New York sure has been good to you. Man, oh man."

"What do you mean?" I ask.

"You look so good," he says. "You look really hot."

In a pleasant way, I say that I'm exhausted and ask him to leave, but I feel angry and lie in bed. Various friends of my mother's poke their heads into my room and try to say something. Mostly, they say, "Oh, Chandler."

That night, after everyone has left, my mom gives me two sleeping pills. She has already taken two herself and is drowsy. She climbs into bed with me and holds my arm and says, "He did this for you and for me. It was an act of love." She runs a hand through my hair. "We'll never have to worry about money again."

The next morning I read a photocopy of my father's suicide letter. The police have the original. It's written only to my mother and says that he loves her and me, but he cannot face financial ruin. He says that his insurance policy will pay a million dollars, and that she can pay the bank the four hundred thousand owed, and that the house will be free and clear with six hundred thousand left over, which should be enough for us to be all right. He says that his body will be in the warehouse and for my mother to call Phil Conti, a friend of my father's who is also a lawyer, and for my mother *do not go down there*. He says that at his office will be instructions regarding the policy and the will and that Phil Conti will handle everything.

The warehouse used to belong to my grandfather, who made his money from real estate. It's an enormous place divided into sections that are rented out to various businesses for storage. The clearest memory I have of my grandfather is watching him play the eighteenth hole at Hardscrabble. I'm walking past the golf course toward the tennis courts with my friends, and I tell them, "Watch this. That's my grandfather, but he won't recognize me." I yell over and wave at him, and he looks back at me with no recollection. I laugh and my friends laugh, and we keep walking.

There is an office right as you go into the warehouse, and I keep picturing my father walking in, sitting in a chair, placing the butt of a shotgun on the floor and the barrel in his mouth and pulling the trigger.

The funeral plans have been made, but there is still the matter of picking out a casket. I go down to the cemetery with Phil Conti. It was his son, I learn now, who drove me to the airport. I have only met Phil Conti a couple of times and don't remember that he's from New York. He tells me about growing up in Brooklyn and ending up in Arkansas because of his wife. We talk about Manhattan, and he says that his mother is in a nursing home in the Village on Hudson Street, close to where I live. Phil Conti has a terrific Brooklyn accent. I love Phil Conti, feel grateful to him, and think I will go visit his mother.

There is a brochure with different caskets at different prices. I'm almost certain that I remember my father saying he wanted to be cremated, but I don't say anything. Phil Conti picks out a mid-priced coffin. The funeral director asks if I want to reserve a plot for myself, so that the Carey family can all be buried together.

"No, thanks," I say.

The funeral director says there's not much space left in the mausoleum, which holds Louis Carey, Marie Carey, Ann Carey, and Don Carey, my father's parents, sister, and brother. "Maybe you would like to start another family area outside by some trees," he says. "Or if you like, you could be cremated, and space would be saved because we could put an urn in the same slot, and that's a lot cheaper."

I ask if they could cremate my father, but he says that it's too late, the mortician is already working on him, and of course, it will be a closed casket. Phil Conti tells the guy that we will stick with what we have, and the mausoleum is fine, and thank you very much.

"God, that was horrible," I say in the car home, and Phil Conti smiles, and I laugh a little.

Later that day, Phil Conti brings over the clothes my father was wearing when he shot himself. He got them from the police station. They are in a brown paper bag—a plaid shirt, tan pants, black socks, Nike tennis shoes, and a Timex watch. They have a certain smell to them. It isn't the smell of blood, or of something rotten. It is the smell of guns, and the smell my father had after he went hunting and was cleaning quail.

My mother reminds me that I must send the airline a copy of the death certificate to get some credit for the twelve hundred dollar ticket home. She says, "Phil Conti has been so nice to us, and we must get this taken care of right away." I nod. "And from now on," my mother says, "we're going to be smart about money."

Even though there is a full house with friends and people from the church with casseroles, my mother and I go down to my father's law office. Mom says we should start cleaning it out, but I know what we are really doing is looking for clues. My mom looks through his files. I look in his desk drawers and find his life insurance policy with a highlighted section that confirms it will pay off on a suicide if the policy is held for three years. His policy is twenty years old. He got it when he was thirty-six, after surviving a heart attack. I remember growing up all we ever ate were chicken and fish and skim milk and margarine and wheat germ and cantaloupe. I remember my dad getting heart medicine delivered every week and meditating with a special word that he wouldn't tell anyone, doing whatever he could to stay alive.

The next morning, my mother and I ride to the funeral in the back of a limousine, and she points out to me all the prominent people of the community. She even rolls down the window and waves at some of them. I bow my head and put my hand over my eyes.

"Can you believe all these people are here for Ben?" my mother says. "I don't think he had any idea how many people loved him."

The chapel is packed, and there isn't enough room for everyone. "I hope they all sign the guest book," my mother says. "Oh, I sure hope so, too," I say. My mother gives me a look.

During the service, the minister lists off my father's accomplishments, but then focuses on his suicide, before saying that we should not remember his death but his life.

At the cemetery, outside the mausoleum, there is a receiving line with my mother and me shaking hands and thanking everyone for coming. There are people I know and people I don't know and don't want to know. What a performance I'm giving and giving. I meet the mayor. "Thanks for coming," I say. I meet my mother's book club friends. "Thanks for coming," I say. "Thanks for coming." I meet cousins of my father's whom I've heard of but have never seen, and when I look into their faces and speak, I can see my father and myself, and I want so badly to be back home in Manhattan.

～

In New York at night, in the darkness before sleep, I lie in bed and look through the bedroom door for my father. It seems as likely a place as any he would show up. He could peer around the corner, say Good night, or Hello, or Everything all right? If I squint my eyes, I can see an outline of him in the pajamas, robe, and tennis shoes he wore around the house when I was growing up. He normally wore a suit to work, but he thought that when you were at home and with your family, you should be comfortable.

Several months ago, during Christmas break, when I was home in Arkansas, my father and I played a lot of gin rummy. He would say, "Cut them thin, so Ben can win." It was something he said when I was young and first learning to play cards. Yesterday I heard the word gin on television and fell apart. Something like that, and I fall into tears, and another day passes.

On television and in movies, there are always people threatening to kill themselves. There are jokes and storylines about insurance policies not paying off on suicides. I know that they do. I want to scream out that they do. And my friends say, "I wanted to kill myself," and don't realize what they've said. They have no idea what is inside me.

When we talk on the phone, my mother makes me promise that I will not kill myself. My mother says if I won't, then she won't either. My mother says, "Now, let's keep our promise to each other." I agree, but it seems crazy that we would say this at all.

My father is the reason that I'm in New York and in law school, and his money will make it easier for me to stay. But it's hard to go to class. I make myself. I can sit through lectures fine. If I get called on, I say, "I don't know." I spend afternoons wandering around Times Square, among tourists, everyone unsure of where to walk next.

I walk to the Ambassador Theater where *Bring in 'Da Noise, Bring in 'Da Funk* is playing. It stars Savion Glover. I've seen him dance before, when I was twelve years old, on a trip here with my father.

The musical is in previews, and I am able to buy a matinee ticket, a good one in the orchestra, maybe because I'm by myself. I wander back into Times Square and wait for the show to begin.

The theater is old, with an orchestra and mezzanine. The ceiling is a gray-blue, and a glass chandelier hangs down. The seats are violet. I'm on the fourth row. The curtain is deep red. The beginning isn't seen but heard. There are taps, and it is dark, and then there is light on the dancer's feet, more taps that grow faster, and then there are other sounds, other feet, other dancers. There are drummers. There is a singer. There is a speaker. And being here so close to the dancer, Savion, I feel a charge, and a current runs through my heart, and I am happy, and I won't let myself look at anyone but him because I don't want my happiness to leave.

Some days I fall into fits of hard crying. My shoulders shake, and I scream and feel out of breath. Then I stop myself, even though I'm alone, because somehow I feel like a fake. I am carrying on this big act of grief, and I feel ashamed for putting on such a show. I know I am sad, but the sadness sometimes reaches an evenness. It isn't always outrage.

The week before my father died, I called home to talk to my mother. My father answered the phone, and I hung up. I felt startled. He never answered the phone. Whenever I was home visiting and the phone would ring, neither of us would answer. It drove my mom crazy, but my father and I would look at each other and smile, co-conspirators.

I remembered right when he said hello that it was my mother's book club night, and that she wouldn't be there. I know he would have had fun talking to me, once we started talking, but always, in the beginning of conversations, we didn't know what to say to each other, as if we were anyone else we'd meet in the course of a day.

I want to go back to that phone call. I want to say, "Don't do it. Don't leave me yet. You are more than money." I at least want to speak this time.

How did he feel that early morning, walking down the stairs, leaving our house, the house he also grew up in, for the last time? Was he crying? Did he pet our cocker spaniel on the way out like he did every other morning?

⇌

Savion pushes up on one toe and stays. I don't even know where his other foot is. Normally he's on one toe and the other is tapping around him. What I like most about coming here is seeing the differences in each performance. He dances in front of a bank of mirrors, and this time he is louder, his taps heavier. He does different steps. At the end of the solo, he falls to the floor in exhaustion. A woman from the mezzanine yells, "Oh, Savion." He stands up quickly and looks in her direction and grins.

Savion is changing tap dancing, changing Broadway. He will be remembered. He matters.

When Savion taps he hardly looks at or faces the audience. He wears loose black pants, an old T-shirt. His shoulders slump a little. He is in control when he dances, not only with movement, but with sound, and somehow with emotion. When I'm watching, and hearing the taps, I'm right with him, and I feel like I can do, am doing, what he's doing. We are in this together, and he knows I need him. He must know that.

Seeing the musical is helping me. It is because of Savion that I get out of bed, leave my room, talk to anyone. It is because I know I can see him dance again. I can see him Tuesday night and then again Saturday matinee. He is someone I have come to depend on.

My father used to send me checks in the mail and write, "To cover a

124

few matinees." He would say that if you see a good musical, you walk out feeling like a million bucks. Despite everything, I still like that expression because my father said it.

The tears are light and slow, but they are always near. They come to me now as I'm sitting in the back of a cab, watching out the windows, looking at buildings and people on Sixth Avenue. I am jealous of girls with fathers, of families, of any two people walking together.

I reach into my purse for the picture of my father I carry with me. It was taken when he was twenty-six here in New York at a law firm party. I hold it in my hand, a beautiful faded color with a white jagged border. My father stands in a circle with the other young associates. He looks strong and handsome and happy to be where he is.

The cab takes me past Macy's and Bryant Park, moving closer to the familiar turn on West Forty-Ninth Street. I put the picture back in my purse, and I don't feel as sad because I know he was good, and was alive, and was my father.

People say I am like my father. I am smart and kind. I am a good tennis player. I am nice looking. I also like staying home. I like to wear pajamas any time of the day.

When I go to see Savion, I prefer to go alone. When I went once with friends, they said, "Oh, it was good. Have you seen this other play? It's good, too." Even Sarah wasn't visibly moved, and I felt lost that even she could not understand that what we were witnessing was amazing.

The cab drops me at Forty-Ninth and Broadway, and I walk the half block west to the Ambassador. I always get a thrill walking this small stretch, seeing others dressed up, rushing to the same theater. I'm not alone at all, and I don't have to speak or shake a hand.

My seat is on the third row center, four from the aisle. There is no one yet next to me, and I begin to feel awkward and obvious. It is not until the lights dim and the orchestra begins playing that the usher leads several people down the aisle. Even in the dark, the whole audience sees who they are. A bodyguard, a beautiful woman, and a movie star. And the movie star sits right beside me. I have seen him before, but I don't know his name. Those around me do, and they whisper. At first, I have to make myself not look at the movie star, but then I get caught up in Savion's dancing.

During intermission everyone wants the movie star's autograph, and I feel almost sorry for him. He doesn't know how to respond. To get away from the crowd, I think, he turns to me and asks how I like the show. I say with all the enthusiasm I've ever spoken with that the dancer is the greatest tap dancer in the world, and this play is better than any book I've read or film I've seen.

"Yes, yes," he says.

We are looking at each other and nodding. I say, "I've seen it five times." I hate to say I've seen it more.

"This is my second time," he says.

I smile.

"It's fantastic," he says.

"It's the only thing that makes me feel better," I say.

"Yeah," he says. "Yeah."

On my first trip to New York, my dad had gotten two rooms at the Waldorf that were connected so I could have my own room. I was only twelve. At night, I would sit in front of the window in my pajamas and lean against the glass, and listen to the cars, the sirens, the subway, people talking and laughing, the doorman whistling for a taxi. My parents would watch me and say, "What are you doing?" and I'd answer, "Listening."

We had already seen *Big River* and *Biloxi Blues*, and for our last night, we had tickets to *Cats*. I did not want to see *Cats* no matter how much my mother did or how often she told me they were T.S. Eliot's cat poems. I wanted to see *The Tap Dance Kid* with Savion Glover. I had seen an ad for it, and at the time I was a Michael Jackson freak, and Savion reminded me of Michael as a kid. Savion was about my age and on Broadway, and I wanted to see him. My dad, without too much persuasion, gave up our *Cats* tickets and bought three tickets for *The Tap Dance Kid*. He even got a limousine to take us to the play. Our driver was named Mannie, and I kept his company card on my bulletin board at home for a long time after.

I remember we were three of the very few white people in the audience. The kid on stage was smiling and playing music with his feet. All the dancers had on tuxedos, which I thought was nice. I kept nudging my parents, saying, "Did you see that?" and, "This is incredible." They would smile and look at each other. My father was wearing wire-rimmed glasses, and they moved a little as he smiled and nodded in agreement with me. I knew he didn't like it the way I did, but I let him know that I loved it, and that was all he needed.

After the show, I bought three *Tap Dance Kid* sweatshirts. At school, I wore one and gave the other two to friends. There was the proof all over the school that I had been to New York City.

⁓

I moved to New York two years ago for law school at NYU. I had no money to come here, and my father didn't have it to give to me.

We all sat in the den to discuss my going to school. My father put on his glasses. "I can't take care of my family," he said.

"Everyone takes out loans," I said.

He sat with a legal pad in his lap, writing down figures, adding what he could afford to pay. "I have these two cases," he said. "One of them has to pay big."

The two cases involved personal injury. He was not used to that type of work, waiting for a settlement or a judgment before he could get paid. He was used to billing hours to a corporation and getting paid each month.

When he finally admitted that his law practice was failing and that we were running out of money, my mother found him these cases. The plaintiffs were two of her acquaintances who quickly became good friends. My father didn't have the money or experience to try the cases, so he got the help of a personal injury firm in St. Louis. He felt if they were willing to put up millions of dollars on behalf of his cases, he was sure to win. My father felt his luck was changing. He felt like the cases just fell in his lap.

My mother was sitting next to me, and she said in a pleading voice, "What will we do if they don't? How are we going to live?"

My father's eyes narrowed, and he shook his head. "Don't say that. I can't stand it when you say that."

"How did this happen to us?" my mother said.

I didn't understand that either. We were rich when I was young.

My father was a corporate lawyer. When he was in his twenties, he had worked for a prestigious firm on Wall Street. In Arkansas, he'd worked for the same corporation for twenty years. When it was taken over, he lost his only client. He had one interview to work with a firm in New Orleans, and when he didn't get the job, that was it. He didn't send his resume out again. He told us that he didn't want to move, that he would figure things out. "I can get clients. I don't mind doing wills and divorces. Not to worry," he said. "I'm a winner. Everything will be fine." So for years, my mother and I thought everything was fine.

My mother, who had always lived in Arkansas, said, "I blame you for her wanting to go to New York City. It is all your fault."

At that, my father looked at me and smiled, and I knew we were in this together, and I would be able to go.

⌇

I love the freedom of New York. I can walk around, and no one knows me. No one knows or cares what has happened to me. I can't imagine how my mother is making it back in Arkansas, how she's able to go to the grocery store or the bank, where she is certain to see someone who knows. I feel so lucky to live in Manhattan, and sometimes I even say out loud to my father, "Thank you." Then I feel ashamed. I only think about myself, about being a daughter who has lost her father, not about my mother and what she has lost.

I decide to call and apologize and ask how *she* is, but when my mother answers, I don't say anything and hang up.

Back in the fall, months before my father died, I walked to The Public Theater hoping to see Savion dance. I already knew the musical was sold out. When I had called earlier about a ticket, a woman told me the show was moving to Broadway, and I could see it in April. I walked down to the Public anyway. I wasn't sure why. I knew I didn't have a chance of getting in. And then I saw Savion. He was leaning against the outside brick of the theater, staring out into the street and the sky, smoking a cigarette. I looked at him as if he were a painting, something to be studied. The white of his shirt, his dark hair compared to his lighter skin, his black pants, and his shoes.

I like Times Square. I like the bright lights of the electric signs. I don't mind walking past Peepland or Runway 69. To me, the neon Xs of strip clubs and the yellow arches of McDonald's somehow add to the beauty. My mother was always afraid of walking through Times Square and I was, too, when I first moved here. And it probably isn't entirely smart now, walking around without reason, away from Times Square and into Hell's Kitchen, as day turns to night. But since my father died, I don't feel like anyone can hurt me.

Without intention, I walk down Forty-Ninth, past Broadway, to the Ambassador. A scalper sees me, walks up to me like he knows me, and offers a ticket. I reach into my purse and pay him. I walk to the side door, the one with fewer people, only one ticket taker, and pray the ticket is not fake. Then, at once, I feel someone brush against me, and I look back and see the white T-shirt, and I look up and see the hair, almost in dreads, and I am at his shoulders, and he passes me, and I'm not sure I am appreciating the good fortune of brushing next to the dancer, this man who I believe is saving me.

I don't feel nervous or excited. I don't want to talk to him. I don't feel anything. And when I should feel something, some kind of gratitude, it is too late, and my chance to feel what I should have felt has passed.

After seeing the musical as many times as I have, I want to skip through certain parts. My mind wanders during the songs and the words. Only when the dancer who brushed against me is dancing is my mind where I wish it to be. Only when he is making music with his tap, notes I have never heard, as if he is inventing them at every performance.

What I feel is the smooth slide, tap, scrape, tap, tap, tap, scrape, and I remember looking up at the dancer, and his face is serious and almost sad, tired, not different from mine.

～ ～ ～

So there is my fictional truth—grieving in New York City and feeling saved by Savion Glover.

I began writing this story like a diary on the plane ride home to my father's funeral. I was raw, and my writing was raw, even written in the white spaces of a novel that I loved, *Leaving Las Vegas*. It was about suicide, and I happened to have just read it. I made these spontaneous notes because I didn't want to have to write later from memory. I somehow knew then what I am certain of now: the more you remember something the less accurate it becomes, and all you have is your most recent recollection. I wanted something pure.

During that time, I was also playing tennis at Manhattan Plaza Racquet Club, on a hard court, on top of a high-rise, close to the Theater District. I'd sometimes think of my tennis shoes like tap shoes. I'd think, "You gotta hit it." This was a phrase I'd heard Savion say. So I'd try to "hit it" with my shoes—small, but loud steps on the court that were in rhythm with my racquet.

Now I work as a teaching tennis pro, and I finally have feet like a lot of professional players. I've had toenails come off and blisters on every toe and calluses on the sides and heels. One of my best tennis students, who now plays college tennis in Miami, said, astonished, "You're just now getting those? Tennis player feet are like dancer feet." I realized then that I was finally "hitting it" like Savion.

I've seen Savion dance a few more times since the year my father died. The most memorable was in 2008—twelve years after I saw him in *Bring in 'Da Noise, Bring in 'Da Funk*—when he played with the great jazz musician McCoy Tyner at The Blue Note. I was by myself. Savion was tap dancing on stage, wildly but controlled, his head down, with his dreadlocks flying, in loose black pants and a black T-shirt. McCoy Tyner was on piano—one hand constant while the other did more complicated patterns. Ravi Coltrane—John Coltrane's son—was on saxophone. Other greats were playing, too. I was blown away by their genius improvisation. Savion clearly felt at home here.

Afterward, I stood across West Third Street on the McDonald's side and waited for Savion to come out the front door of The Blue Note. While I waited, when the traffic cleared, a crazy, homeless-looking man would go out into the street and hit smashed tin cans with a golf club. I also watched a rat go from the fence of the basketball court that faced Sixth Avenue to the piles of big black trash bags where there were old fries leaking out from one of them. The rat would take one at a time back to wherever he lived. My eyes went back and forth from the tin-can golf to the rat and fry, then finally I saw Savion, dreads tucked into a wool cap, his thin frame hidden under a thick black coat.

He was joyous, smiling, swaying, then waving goodbye to McCoy Tyner who got into a Cadillac town car with his driver, a dapper white-haired man who looked like he was in the mob and who had done on Thursday night—when my friend Dee and I were there, watching him from the bar through a window—a dance in the rain—just for us—with his black felt hat and raincoat and long umbrella. Savion stood in front of McCoy Tyner's window and smiled and waved at him again. It was a sweet scene.

Watching Savion, I felt almost invisible, with my puffer coat and fur-lined hood covering my blond hair. I thought of myself as a middle-aged stalker—thirty-eight at the time. Savion had on a big backpack and didn't look as tall off the stage. I followed him at a safe distance a few blocks to his car on Sullivan Street.

I just wanted to be in his presence a while longer, but I couldn't bring myself to catch up to him and speak to him and thank him. Instead, I held up my arm for an oncoming cab and hoped that I hadn't scared him.

I know from an editor that his mother requested a copy of this story when it was first published as nonfiction, in a Manhattan newspaper. Then part of that story was published in *A Secret Word* and in the *New York Times* as fiction. Then I was part of a story on grieving in the *New York Times* called "Mourning Rooms." My mourning room was the theater. And here the story is again.

And so surely Savion knows by now that he saved some woman through an awful time. And maybe he knows that her father—even though he committed suicide—was a nice man, a pure spirit. And maybe Savion even knows that just the memory, her malleable memory, of his shoes and their tap, tap, tap, scrape, smooth slide, saves her still.

❧ OLD HEADS ❧

by Bay Woods

J.R. Gordon was my state appointed drug counselor; his methods were extreme, immoral, and highly illegal, but they were the only ones that could have worked for a guy like me, and in writing this, I know I am breaking his first rule, the first rule of all old heads, the only rule that mattered, the breaking of which leads only to despair or death.

"When asked if you do drugs," J.R. would say like a balding smash-faced preacher to our unruly band of fuck-ups sitting on the carpeted floor of a room in the State Commission of Alcohol and Drug Abuse and we would all liturgically respond: "Just Say No!"

There were two brothers who had stolen a Miller beer truck and parked it in their mother's driveway and drank the beer from the back until they passed out; another guy chained a Coke machine to the back of his pickup truck so he could steal the change, but it slipped as he was driving past a cop and sent a rooster tail of sparks onto the street.

And me?

It was the last day of midterm exams in the eleventh grade, the day before a long weekend. I'd already failed my chemistry class for the year; I had so many zeroes that it was mathematically impossible to pass. So I had an early dismissal. The unseasonably warm January day was full of promise as I bought a quarter bag of weed that morning. The future was mine.

I left with three guys from the school—they weren't friends of mine but they smoked weed and one of them had sold me the bag. We went and drank warm beer and kicked a hackeysack as we smoked a bowl in the parking lot of a neighborhood pool. Driving back to school, one of them threw a white Burger King bag out the window. A silver and black storm-trooper looking patrol car pulled up behind me just as I was driving past the school and pulled me over into the parking lot.

A cop pulled me from the car just as three more cars pulled up, all of their lights flashing for the entire student body milling about in the commons outside the building.

After they found the bag of weed in my pocket, one of the deputies handcuffed me while another conferred with the vice principal. The first cop got on his megaphone. He grabbed me by the scruff of the neck and said, "Everyone, look at your friend, look at your peer. See what drugs will do to you." He pushed me into the back of the car and my life was suddenly part of an after school special.

Part of that was counseling. I got into pretrial intervention and had to go to counseling at the State Commission of Alcohol and Drug Abuse in a desolate section of town across the parking lot from the old bowling alley.

J.R. Gordon was a short and stocky guy with a smashed nose and a knotty pink balding head. The little bit of white hair he had, he let grow into a founding father ponytail to protest the first Iraq war. But that was a little later.

J.R. once told me that he had loved a girl, but she was rich and her father told him he was linthead trash and would never have her.

He went to Vietnam as a Conscientious Objector, so they put him in the Red Cross "which meant you had a red target on your head and no gun as you was flying into battle to pick up the wounded and the dead," as he put it. He came back, became a hippie, went to college, grew weed and took acid, got into coke, got clean, and became a drug counselor.

Half the time our counseling consisted of sitting around telling stories about times we'd been really fucked up, which seems to be the chief pleasure of counseling. None of us were older than eighteen. We weren't like the grizzled dudes in AA who have done enough shit to scare themselves when they talk about it. We were ready for more.

J.R. must have been about thirty-seven or thirty-eight at the time. One night he told us that he had taken acid the previous weekend. "An old buddy came down and we were walking around my farm and he gave me a drink and he'd put a hit in it."

J.R. grinned so that we couldn't tell if he was serious or not. It sounded like a parody of the kind of bullshit excuses we told our parents.

After I'd been in counseling for a year, J.R. showed us the first part of *Easy Rider* and let us go early. I stood on the concrete balcony with a kid named Sam who had been in the group as long as me. We were smoking in the cold and we started talking about how great it would be to get high. "Let's see if J.R. has something," one of us said. It was absurd, but we convinced each other we should try.

We walked back into the Commission of Alcohol and Drug Abuse and into our counselor's office. He was sitting at his desk over some papers. "J.R.," I said. "We were wondering if you wanted to smoke with us."

"Why, you got something?" he said, looking up from the papers.

"No, we were hoping you did," was my outrageous reply. And yet...

He leaned back and grinned, his deep blue eyes sparkling in the frame of the bit of white hair around his ears. Then he got up. "Come on," he said. He took me and Sam down to his car and sure enough, he came out with a tiny joint. He handed it to me. "Next week, you both tell your parents that you're graduating after the session and that you'll be out late."

We staggered away, bowled over by the size of our own balls, first and foremost because we were of that age, we who had asked our drug counselor for weed which he had thereupon given unto us so that Ask-and-Ye-Shall-Receive-like blessedness hovered about our shoulders and we were so absorbed by this great gift and the mystery of the size of our own balls and the blessedness of our own lives that as we sat there inside the car, fogging it out, we hardly even bothered to marvel at this man, this utter enigma, there was no way we could understand, we did not wonder about him because we could not see beyond ourselves and it seemed natural that some old dude would want to get high with us, but it also cracked something open right there that night, revealing most importantly unto me that I had been fucking right and that all the motherfuck-

ing adults were bullshit liars in a fucked-up conspiracy and one, this one, had finally somehow told the truth and half of my trouble in the suburban Southern world in which I was raised was that I wanted to be a poet and fancied myself a storyteller and though my mother is very much a mystic, she also has very material, commercial—of the shopping mall variety—interests and she was embarrassed that I didn't seem like a nice Polo-wearing Christian boy and my dad probably thought it despicable that I hated cars, hated sports, and had no interest in business or finances, but I wouldn't let them forget my differences anymore, not as I had for years and years during the early part of my life, before I discovered skateboarding when at school, when I was simply one of the less-cool kids, I was not a jock and I had not yet found another cool that was not the mainstream cool, but when I did I felt free, girls finally paid attention to me, and I overcame the debilitating uncoordination that had plagued me, so when I could rebel I felt compelled to do it constantly and consistently, and more than any of my friends, and yet, when I did, I also always felt the utter alienation of going too far, the alienation of the law, where you are not part of a group, are not friends with anyone, you are your name and your future and your past standing completely exposed and alone where no one can answer for you, handcuffed and hauled away from school, the way my mother looked down at me and sobbed as she came into the police station to get me that day, but, though I didn't know my motivations then and am certainly not in a knowledgeable or objective position to do so over twenty years later, that certainly was part of the point, and so I was stuck in a bind of having this great story, the story to end all stories and prove that I was all along fucking right, the story of getting high with my drug counselor, the silence that the true vindication recalled because I would have the best story ever but I could not tell it.

The next week, we watched the rednecks kill Jack Nicholson, Dennis Hopper, and Peter Fonda. All the other kids left, and J.R. and Sam and I went down to J.R.'s car. He told me to pull mine up beside it. He opened the trunk. There was a cooler full of beer. "You're driving," he said, and we hoisted the cooler into my car. Sam got in the back. He had a half-ounce. So did J.R. They were rolling joints and packing bowls simultaneously as I drove. We threw beer cans out the window and they clanked in the empty streets of our own redneck town as we blasted rock and roll.

I remember stopping three times for J.R. to go in and buy another twelve-pack. I don't remember getting home at 4:00 a.m.

After that night, Sam was done, but the "Just Say No" program was working for me—smoothing things over with my parents, at least. I became, in a very informal way, an assistant counselor, helping J.R. run the group for the new kids.

After the meetings, we often went out and drove around, smoking bowls and drinking beer. He told me that he was going through a divorce. He said that his wife wanted to be normal and to grow up, but that he felt like he was still a "freak," in the sixties parlance. "I'm just an old head," he said. "And that will never change."

When I brought my deadhead girlfriend to meet him, J.R. liked her immediately. He went to the store and bought a bunch of beer and we ended up wasted, smoking cigarettes and drinking beer and drawing on the chalkboard of our counseling room in the State Commission for Alcohol and Drug Abuse. She drank too much and went running off screaming through the night. It was raining and J.R. and I staggered around the parking lot and up the sidewalk screaming, "Lucy!" We eventually found her, but it is a miracle that no one found us.

Again I don't know how I got home.

One night, I showed up for the counseling and J.R. asked me if I would run it. I was going to show half of *River's Edge* and then talk about it with the group. Afterward, I went into his office.

"I need you to do me a favor," he said. "I got a note to meet someone at Cleveland Park. Only I don't know if she wrote the note or if someone is trying to trap me."

"Okay," I said. He explained that he was seeing a woman and her estranged husband was back in town.

He lay in the back of my car when I got to the park. I drove by the appointed spot— a certain picnic table by a parking area. There was a man there. "What does he look like?" J.R. asked.

"I don't know," I said.

"What kind of car? Is it big, burgundy?"

"No."

"Drive by again," he demanded, cramped down in the back of the car. I drove by three times.

The movie River's Edge *became a touchstone in our conversation—he was like Dennis Hopper's character "Fec" and I, alas, was Crispin Glover, careening about town maniacally obsessed with my friends, and we called his weed "fec-weed," and that night it didn't seem yet like J.R. was unraveling or this situation was perhaps as deranged as the one in the movie but now, twenty years later, now that I am forty, I can't understand him anymore than I did then, I can't imagine how tedious, as well as dangerous, it would be to go out drinking and drugging with a couple seventeen year olds, except that, then I was an expert at burning down my life and perhaps J.R. wanted that from me, he wanted to burn down his own life, burn all the miles he had walked, the place unto which his life had brought him, burning it down and if he could not burn those miles he could at least symbolically burn the joints we passed in the car, like a bag of shoes on a cold night, smoldering to maintain the proper warmth for drinking, as the writer Everett Capps did one night in Alabama, where he wrote the book* Off Magazine Street *in which a couple of old drunks and reprobates educate a young woman despite their own failings, drunkenness, and lechery, and I think that J.R. played a similar but opposite role in my life, becoming a true teacher only when he fell from grace, only when he demolished his official role and the rules of his profession and I know I could never do that, sacrifice myself in that way, that I wouldn't have the desperation, the patience, or the courage, and I know that, somehow, despite his admittedly insane failings, J.R. was more of a man than I am, that at some level, Christlike, he sacrificed himself for me and I thought of him years later, when I became obsessed with Buddhism and went to a Zen monastery for intense meditation but was seduced by a nun, was drunkenly fucked by her, and shaken out of my Buddhist trance so that when I took the Bodhisattva vow, promising that I would not be enlightened until all beings had achieved Nirvana, I knew I would never practice Buddhism again, that in order to fulfill the vow I couldn't, and I thought of J.R. because if he had been caught as we drove around in my Volkswagen as we smoked a bowl and drank beers, the events that would have necessarily unfolded would have burned his life completely, inescapably and he would have to stay there watching it like that pair of shoes, and perhaps it was that anticipation—the way destruction can seem so delicious— that kept the stupid chatter of this seventeen-year-old from tiring this older man because the promise that he would be arrested and ridiculed and shamed was appropriately apocalyptic.*

A couple weeks later, I drove down to Florida with some friends to pick mushrooms from a cow pasture. We were stopped in Houston County, Georgia, and locked up and shackled and handcuffed to a bench.

Twenty-four hours later, we were finally charged with simple possession of marijuana because of the resin in the bowl. They tore the seats out of the car but never found our real weed (hidden in the leather around the gearshift). They didn't charge us with the mushrooms because their crime lab was closed on the weekend.

J.R. was the first person I called. "J.R., can I borrow five hundred dollars?"

I told him where I was.

"I'll call your parents and make it easier."

Bail was my graduation present.

Clearly, I couldn't be assistant counselor anymore. Still, when I got back, I met up with J.R. one night. We smoked a bowl. "Look. Your parents are freaked," he said. "They don't know what to do with you. But the world can handle you. Just get done and get out of there. It's only two more months," he said. He called my doctor and got me Ritalin.

Eventually, I did finish high school and shortly after that J.R. lost his job, apparently because of the affair he was having with the mother of two clients—the woman he wanted me to look for at the park.

My girlfriend and most of my high school friends went on tour with the Grateful Dead that summer. I couldn't do that. I couldn't follow. I was alone and free to reinvent.

I got kicked out of my parents' house when they found a woman they'd never seen in my bed. Her name was Pearl and she was a writer and a stripper and she let me live with her.

Strippers were always around us with drugs. We went to bed in the morning and woke up in the evening. Pearl had gone to college and studied with James Dickey. She claimed she quit, a semester before graduating, when a professor said, "Poetry is the dung heap upon which the flower of criticism grows." I was supposed to be taking classes at the tech school, but wasn't.

At first we'd lived with one of her co-workers and her boyfriend, but eventually we moved into a duplex my grandfather owned. We were supposed to pay rent, but rarely did.

The house was a two-bedroom brick thing in a swampy yard in a mill village. We had a tremendous wooden bed with a frame that was hung with red velvet curtains and we spent much of our time in it. We'd been up on acid all night and it was about eight in the morning and the birds were chirping when there was a knock.

The roaches scurried into the empty beer cans littering the floor as

I stumbled through the trash and looked out the window and saw that it was my mom and a carpet installer named Dale. I'd worked as an assistant to him a couple summers before. When his wife left him and took the kids, he drove his van through the wall of her mother's house. That's the kind of guy he was.

I was confused.

Dale had come in to fix the toilet a few days back. He'd found a rolled-up dollar bill. "I know cocaine," he said.

"We have not been snorting cocaine," I said truthfully, without adding that we had been snorting Ritalin. "I don't have the money to buy a cheeseburger. How would I buy coke?"

"You got the flophouse, you don't need money," he said, my mom standing weirdly in the background, fidgeting with her fingers.

"I don't have to do anything, and I don't even know why I'm talking to you—why did you bring him, Mom? What the hell is this?—but I'll piss in a cup to show you we haven't been doing cocaine," I said. I stormed into the kitchen. I grabbed a Van Gogh coffee mug. I took out my dick and pissed in it. I came back wielding it proudly.

"You can have any kid pee for you," Dale said, seeming to puff himself up in front of me. He wasn't a big guy but he was tough, with the kind of wiry strength that comes from forty years of physical labor. His eyes were wild and his mullet haircut hung down over his denim shirt.

"And I just happen to have one back there, in waiting? It's warm," I said. "You want to feel?"

He stepped forward to say something just as I threw the cup. It spun through the air and hit the coffee table, breaking and splashing a warm spray of urine on a copy of Emerson's essays—and on Dale.

He lunged forward and grabbed me by the hair.

He threw me into the front door. I bounced off it but he still had me by the hair and slammed me into it again. He opened the door and tossed me out onto the porch. I hit the light first and then the concrete with a searing thud. He grabbed me by the hair again and the arm and slung me down the stairs into the swampy yard. He banged my head into a ditch surrounding the yard. My nose filled with ditchwater. My eyes went blind with mud. I choked and coughed when he pulled me back by my hair so he could smash my face once again into the sodden earth as my Mom's screams echoed as the vague background of the slurry of pain and mud that filled the moment.

And then everything stopped. It was quiet except for the pain in my face and my gasping for breath. Dale still held me by the back of the hair, but he wasn't moving anymore.

I coughed and spit up water and looked up through the mud and blood and saw Pearl standing there wearing nothing but a fur coat and a cowboy hat, pointing a BB gun at Dale.

Maybe she was wearing boots, too, but they weren't cowboy boots, but stripper boots, thigh-high, and that's the way I like to see it in my mind, everything frozen there like that, my mom standing off to the side in mid scream, my head in the hand of the carpet installer all staring at my girlfriend naked with gun and boots and a fur coat.

I tasted the blood in my mouth. I grabbed a lead pipe lying in the yard. My mom grabbed Dale by the arm and tried to get him into her car as I threatened to break his fucking head as much to save my pride as for any physical desire for revenge.

Later that night J.R. pulled up in our drive. He came back to our room, where I was lying, my face swollen. He pulled out one of his pin joints and lit it up. He had a forty in a paper bag. He passed me the joint, took a big slug of beer, and pulled out a sheet of paper.

"Look what I got today at my new job," he said. I couldn't tell what the paper said, because he was waving it around. He looked older, but was also more antic, more spastic, and on fire. "It's the paperwork to have you committed to the loony bin for thirty days of mental evaluation," he said.

"My mom brings a maniacal carpet installer over to kick my ass and I'm the one who gets committed?" I said, stunned.

He ripped up the paper with a flourish. The pieces fell onto the sheets of the bed. He lit another pin joint.

And from that ripping paper and that flourish of the pin joint the next twenty years flowed, all because J.R. trusted me and helped me escape the institutions that the world in Greenville, South Carolina felt I needed and he kept me free so we could escape from the town shortly after and live in a VW van as we travelled from city to city, stopping first at the strip club wherever we ended up, me driving, her dancing, and that too was precisely the education I needed before I ended up in New Mexico where I no longer had South Carolina to rebel against and actually went to college and learned things and did the kinds of things that prove J.R.'s theory right, proved that it did work, that he somehow saved my life, that despite the literary custom, I was not a victim of his corruption, that I grew in valuable ways under his tutelage, but I also know that people won't understand that, that his family, my family, all the decent people in all the world will not understand it, but to us old heads that means little compared with the debt that I must repay even if, as a teacher and a department chair for many years, I would have abhorred and castigated and thrown out a man like him, and even though writing this makes me less likely to ever hold such a job again, this debt compels as much honesty as literature is capable of, the kind of honesty full of all the misrememberings that the drugs we took then and the years that have passed since have created, and it is a debt of his silence, and his lies, for it was his lies that have saved me, and his outrages, both from my parents and myself, and I believe I may have died without him so I must repay him in turn and rightly with an outrage of my own, with the breaking of the first rule of old heads and I must tell all of this to you because I know I cannot tell him because he is dead, J.R. Gordon is dead as I discovered last week when my periodic googling of his name finally produced the only search result that is ever and always inevitable—I saw his obituary and I knew I had to just say yes, to say yes, to tell our story because his rule applies only to the living and the walking not to the dead and lying, if they could desire, would, I imagine, desire nothing more than to be remembered for the effects they have had on the living, for the morality of their actions, of all our actions, must be calculated somewhere between intent and outcome, between the inner and the outer, and I know J.R. knew the man he was, knew everything he had done, lived his life in a way I couldn't and can't imagine, and I did not do what my job as a reporter would train me to, I did not call up his ex-wife and try to find out what had become of him in the twenty years since we had last seen one another, and I did not go back to that town to poke around looking for people who knew him in order to recreate his life, nor did I dig up some goofer dust at his grave to cast a spell or bring me luck (I have collected dust from the graves of Ed McTeer, about whom I wrote a book, and the great North Carolina native New Yorker writer Joseph Mitchell), because my luck was obviously terrible when I was around J.R., so he can keep his luck, but still, I turned to memory with this desire to understand what this man has meant to me in my life, so I sat down here with a cold can of beer and set to breaking up marijuana on a Ramones album cover and rolled up a little pin joint and now I take a lighter and I turn the wheel and the flame leaps out and I light it and inhale deeply, trying to get high with a ghost, and in the rolling big cloud of smoke I exhale, I see J.R. Gordon.

SEVEN DAYS

by Bev Marshall

Day One:

   She sits on the floral print cushion of the rattan chair beside the window. She watches the bikini clad sunbathers gathered around the thatch-roofed bar. The men buying their drinks aren't military. She can tell by their haircuts, by the casual carefree way they laugh, throwing their heads back as they slam their dollars on the wooden bar. She wishes she were one of those women whose only thought might be what she'll wear to dinner tonight. She hasn't eaten. She doesn't want to risk mixing food with the butterflies in her stomach. Her next meal will be with him and she plans to order prawns and one of those tropical drinks before she goes back home to Mississippi. Mai Tai, piña colada, the names sound romantic, exotic, like frangipani, Oahu, Kauai, Maui. She's never been so far away from home.

   She checks her hair in the framed mirror over the vanity, pushes a blond strand over her ear. She wasn't a blond when he boarded the plane in New Orleans. She didn't have pierced ears then either. In the nine long months she's been a waiting wife, she's changed many things, and not just her appearance. She's a teacher, a working girl, an apartment dweller with interesting funny neighbors. She'd trade it all for the chance to have her life with him back.

Where is he? Has the plane crashed? Did it land safely without him, and if so, why wasn't he on it? She glances at the bedside clock once more. Seven twelve. He had written he'd be at the hotel by four thirty. She smiles remembering the letter she's folded and refolded so many times that lies beside the Pan American ticket in her purse. She's memorized nearly all of it. *"Finally, I've got R & R, Rest and Recreation, and I'm planning on lots of resting with you lying naked beside me."*

She's wearing navy shorts, a red, white, and navy blouse, with matching sandals—she's a patriot. From head to toe. She'll be one as long as her husband is dodging mortar fire in the plane he flies above the jungles of Vietnam. To hell with hippies. Screw the draft dodgers. She won't listen to their chants. The body count they shout as they ignite their draft cards. He was a volunteer.

She's thinking of changing into the celery green gown she's planned for this night, when she hears the door lock click. He's here. He's safe. She lets out her breath in a whoosh. She runs to his outstretched arms.

Day Two:

Kauai is all she'd dreamed it would be after she read in the brochure that the musical *South Pacific* was filmed here at Hanalei Plantation. She's seen the movie twice and knows all the songs by heart. In fact, she feels like a movie star herself in this beautiful room. The glass wall looks down onto a private cove. White sheers hang from bamboo rods around the bed, and the bathroom vanity is red-veined marble. On the round table overlooking the cove sits a welcome basket of oranges, pineapple, mangos, and bananas.

He jumps on the bed and pats the space beside him. "Come here," he says. "What a view!"

She lies beside him, suddenly shy. It's been such a long time since she's been with a man. When he'd made love to her last night, she'd been someone else. Some fictional woman who knew how to welcome her man home properly. Now she's stuck with who she is and he isn't the familiar man she'd married three years ago. He's a warrior now.

She squeezes her eyes shut as he slides his briefs down his golden-haired legs. When he blows on her flat stomach, her eyes fly open and she laughs as she wiggles away. She sighs when he kisses her quiet.

Day Three:

The orchid on the breakfast plate dazzles her. Orange slices have
never tasted so delicious. He wants to rent a jeep. They will have lunch
on the other side of the island. He drives masterfully on the narrow
roads. She remembers when he raced go-karts in high school. He wanted
to be a Formula One driver, had told her he was going to quit college to
pursue his dream. She'd given back the tiny diamond engagement ring.
"I can't live that life of danger," she'd said. She hadn't imagined he'd be
in danger anyway. The wind whips her hair into her face. She lifts her
face to the sun. She blinks the memories and her fears away. Today he's
here beside her in the speeding jeep. She lays her hand on his leg. She has
him for only four more days.

At the outdoor picnic table she smiles as she watches him hunched
over his food. He says he hasn't tasted anything so good since they'd
eaten at Galatoire's that last night in New Orleans. She thinks of all the
meals they've missed eating together and feels a moment of sadness. She
will follow the advice she'd read in one of the self-help books she'd pur-
chased the week he left. Stay in the present; put aside fears of the future.

Back in their room, they lie side by side on the bed. They talk until
the sun burns down into the ocean. In the semidarkness, he turns to her,
takes her face in his hands. Her eyes fill with grateful water. She's over-
come with loving this man.

Day Four:

They walk along the rocky shoreline. He talks about things he hasn't
written about in his letters. As he tells her about landing on makeshift
strips of land carved out of the jungle, of mortar fire that hits the under-
belly of the Caribou he's piloting, of the Vietnamese he's relocated out of
harm's way, she understands that he has fallen in love with the military.
She can't comprehend these tales of short field landings and flaps and
ailerons, and evasive maneuvers in the sky. When she talks about the
Charles Dickens projects her students have accomplished, his gaze drifts
out toward China. She falls silent and walks ahead. From behind his
arms reach out to encircle her. He pulls her close. "Let's go back to the

room," he says.

She dresses for dinner. She wiggles her breasts into the padded push up bra. The pale pink sundress shimmies down over her body. She slides her feet into strappy pumps and pirouettes; the full skirt billows around her in soft waves. He catches her mid-turn. He whispers, "You're beautiful and sexy." She smiles. He's such a good liar.

She eats the prawns the dignified waiter has set down with a flourish on the patio table. She doesn't know quite how to respond to the waiter's obsequious manner. He doesn't notice the waiter. He's talking with his hands now, flying his palms over his empty plate. He smokes a cigar and the blue smoke drifts into her hair and she thinks that he seems far older than she. He's only twenty-four but he has the eyes of a battle tested soldier. In three days he'll be a soldier again and she'll be boarding a plane back to Mississippi. She ducks her head, takes a breath, and then lifts her eyes to his. "I know," he says.

Day Five:

They lie sated on the white curtained bed. He tells her he is considering making the Air Force his career. She reminds him he'd promised to go back to law school when his commitment was up. He reminds her they'll have loans, debts that will take years to repay. She can have a maid, travel to other countries, retire while they're still young enough to enjoy life. Stay in the military and see the world. "There's a lot more out there than what's in Mississippi," he tells her. He's been dreaming of living in Spain, in Germany, of flying planes that can break the sound barrier. She doesn't tell him that his dreams are her nightmares. She doesn't say that the war has already killed thousands of dreams. She wonders if he believes that God is protecting him. She doesn't know if she believes this herself. Only two days left. Stay in the present, stay in the present, she chants in her head.

Day Six:

They fly to Honolulu, check into the hotel, don their swimsuits, and sprint across the highway to Waikiki Beach. She lays the hotel towel on the sugar-white sand. He has brought his new Canon and snaps shots of her lying on her side in her aqua bikini. "You're so brown," she says. "I hope I can get a little tan before going back to Mississippi."

"Better put on more sun block," he says. "You're really fair-skinned."

An hour on the beach. He's right; the sun seems closer, hotter here than back home. She should suggest they go back to the room. But it's the last day. When this day ends, the time they've been allotted will be spent. Empty wallet, all gone, nothing left. She leans over, her mouth close to his ear. "I love you I love you I love you."

Two hours on the beach. Two hours too long. The blisters rise like bread dough. She shakes with chills.

"I've ruined our last night," she says. It's true. When he puts his arms around her, she cries out in pain. With a groan, he moves to the other side of the bed.

Day Seven:

She opens her eyes and closes them again. She doesn't want this day to begin. She doesn't want to pack her clothes into her new luggage. She doesn't want to go to the airport in Honolulu. She doesn't want him to go back to Saigon. He shakes her. "Time to get going," he says. His eyes are red, puffy. He hasn't slept either. They don't talk as she folds her shorts and tops, as he stuffs his swimsuit into the green duffle bag. They check the drawers, the bathroom shelf, beneath the bed. There is nothing left to pack. It's time to call the cab.

The Pan American gate agent tells them where to go to board the plane that will carry all the men on R&R back to their bases and posts. There will be a short delay. They see the big white and blue plane on the tarmac. She can't guess how many passengers it will hold, but she thinks maybe two hundred. She turns and sees that the waiting room is crowded now.

There are three hundred or more people, men, women, a few children and a couple of babies in this glass-walled room. The men are dressed in uniforms of every branch of the service, a collage of Army green, brown khaki, Air Force blue, Navy white and black. Some of the soldiers can't be more than eighteen, some of the wives even younger. There are no old people in the room. At least one hundred people are already crying, some silently, others moaning. Everyone is kissing, hugging, clinging to someone. An announcement blares out, "Time to board, men. Let's go."

Everyone falls silent. She clings to him for this last kiss, and she knows that many of these women are kissing their husbands for the last time ever. She knows she could be one of them. A young boy drops to a chair and sobs. She hears his wife say, "Don't go. Stay." A soldier pats the young girl's shoulder as he walks by.

She stands watching his back until he disappears. When the door to the jet way closes, the silence in the room is unbearable. She hears her breath, the inhalation of the girl standing next to her. She moves away, almost tiptoeing to the window. She sees the plane sitting on the runway now like a giant bomb that will blow up the lives of the families in this room. She sees the frightened drawn faces at the window. As the women and children watch the plane slowly begin to taxi away, the sound of their breaths can't be heard anymore. They're all holding them in. She watches the plane until it turns onto the taxiway, and she leans her forehead against the glass. It is cool on her sunburn and she feels water running down her leg from the blisters breaking behind her knees. No one leaves the room. Everyone knows that some of them will be widows within months or even weeks. Some of the children in this room won't have a father to toss them a ball, to tuck them into bed, to teach them to drive or swim or fish or share any of life's lessons. She drops down onto a plastic chair; some of the women continue standing at the window as if expecting the plane to reappear. Finally, a baby cries from across the room, and then a torrent of sobs erupts. She sees several girls sink to the floor, two of them pregnant, and she thinks maybe she could be one of them now. Maybe she's carrying an egg inside her womb at this moment and a baby of their own will be the gift of this trip. But somehow she knows that her womb is as barren as her heart, and she picks up her carry-on and walks away from the carnage, the obscenity of war.

 MONK

excerpted from *Katrina Rising*, by Judith Richards

Monk hung his shoes around his neck tied together by laces. He patted his pocket to be sure his harmonica was there, grabbed a floppy straw hat, and then ran to overtake Percy out by the street.

Percy pushed the wheel and Monk trotted alongside until they crossed the canal bridge where bicycling was forbidden. Then Monk climbed on the handlebars and Percy peddled. Four miles to go.

The air was warm on Monk's face. He clamped the hat to his head with one hand, careful not to get his toes in the spokes of the bicycle. Suburban smells gave way to city scents of burnt rubber and automobile fumes. They passed dark dens where zydeco pulsed from open doorways. In another building half a block farther, the recorded music of Fats Domino lured customers into a bar where men drank beer for breakfast and played bourré.

Percy maneuvered around abandoned cars and over broken curbing. He took back alleys and side streets to avoid the hangout of thugs who charged a fee to let them pass. From the Lower Ninth Ward they went through Bywater and Faubourg Marigny to the Quarter.

"Got your come money?" Percy spoke over Monk's shoulder.

"I got it." He kept four one-dollar bills to sweeten the pot.

When tourists saw paper money in a hat, they tended to donate in kind. Loose change invited more coins.

At thirteen, Percy was four years older than Monk, taller, stronger, and more nearly the color of Grandmama's dark complexion than Monk's cinnamon tan. Percy was a better dancer and played a mean bone. Tourists enjoyed him but held onto their money, and that's where Monk came in.

He couldn't blow the mouth harp as well as Percy, and he certainly couldn't make sparks fly with his homemade taps. But he was small and looked younger than his nine years. Percy taught him to "sell" the act. Grinning and thrashing, tapping and whooping, sucking and blowing the M. Hohner Marine Band harmonica Monk played while Percy kept time with slaps and claps.

They were a team in holey clothes, wearing scuffed shoes and twine-bound trousers. When they were home practicing together, Grandmama sat on the back steps and coached them. She knew show business. "Yelp and holler," Grandmama tutored. "Knee-slap and clickety-clack with those taps. If people laugh out loud, they'll part with their money."

There were days when they made fifty or sixty dollars.

Percy hit a pothole and Monk was nearly unseated. "Sorry, Monk."

It hurt his tailbone, but Monk said, "I'm okay."

⁓

Sooner or later every visitor to New Orleans ended up in Vieux Carré, known the world over as the French Quarter. Monk enjoyed walking past window displays of Mardi Gras masks and vulgar bumper stickers. In the evening, hawkers stood on the banquette tempting passersby with descriptions of floorshows inside. But for now, the bawdy houses had not begun to open. Monk was seldom here at night because Grandmama expected him home before dark, and anyway, cops chased him off. At sundown Bourbon Street closed to motor traffic and only pedestrians were allowed. At that point, the Quarter was not for children.

Someday, when he was a grown man, Monk planned to explore those forbidden places that Grandmama called dens of iniquity. Percy had already been inside. He'd been everywhere. One of his aunts ran a voodoo shop on Toulouse, half a block off Bourbon. If the police caught Percy wandering, he told them he was going to see his aunt and they let him through. A second aunt was a bishop at the Blessed Baby Jesus Spiritual Church. In her company Percy was allowed to be present because where the bishop went was God's will. His aunt, Bishop Beulah, once saved a naked stripper who was halfway up a rubbing pole when she got the calling and went into rapture right there on the stage. Percy was a witness.

Bicycling through gathering tourists, Percy predicted, "Going to be good crowds today. Be hot, but good crowds."

The Quarter was a magical place. Street musicians produced energetic melodies from guitars, accordions, and homemade percussions. Clowns and robotic mimes performed on every corner. Newly washed streets smelled faintly of garbage, but overriding that came the odor of beignets and coffee from Café Du Monde. Lucky Dog vendors pushed their carts up and down nearby streets offering steamed wieners. Restaurants served Cajun and French foods that contributed exotic aromas of baked fish with garlic sauce and crawfish étouffée. Over it all wafted the malty smell of spilled beer.

Rising from the center of the square, General Andrew Jackson sat astride a rearing horse, his hat held high as if to acknowledge cheers from a grateful population. In 1814 he defeated the British and saved the city during the Battle of New Orleans. The square was named in his honor.

Monk knew these things because the historian, Quinton Toussaint, had told him.

"There's the old queer now," Percy sneered.

"Don't call him that, Percy. He's our friend."

"He ain't my friend, Monk. You're the one he wants to do."

"He doesn't do anything."

"One of these days he might."

Quinton wore green seersucker trousers, a ruffled canary yellow shirt, and a hat decorated with long feathers dyed the colors of Mardis Gras, purple, green, and gold. When he saw them coming, he stood up. At the age of eighty-two, he was ten years older than Grandmama, but whereas her weight made Grandmama move slowly, Quinton was thin and spry.

"There you are, boys! I thought I'd have to trip the terpsichore in your absence this morning." Monk didn't always understand what he said. Quinton's voice was high tenor, and he spoke with a lilting delivery, as if about to sing every sentence.

"Miss James made us eat breakfast before Monk could leave," Percy explained.

"As indeed she should," Quinton said. "May I help with your shoes, Monk?"

"I got them."

Percy was ready, testing his new taps with a heel, toe, and slide. Monk envied the crisp clicks and sparks he created.

Quinton spoke to passing strangers. "They'll be performing shortly. The best act in New Orleans." He pronounced the name of the city "Nawlins."

Monk placed his straw hat on the pavement, positioned dollar bills for best effect, and stepped away ready to dance.

They began with body slaps and toe taps, creating a rhythm that made people pause to listen. Monk blew full-mouth on his harmonica, suck-n-blow, suck-n-blow, followed by handclaps and steady taps, holding the cadence. Then Percy yielded the rhythm and tongued his harp down to a single quavering note, with a double tongue beat. A melody established, the music gathered listeners. Monk jumped into motion, tapping, grinning, and slapping his chest in time to Percy's harmony.

"Do it like the Spirit's on you," Percy counseled. He'd learned that from his aunt Bishop Beulah. "Move where the Spirit says go!"

Tap-a-dap, heel and toe, long slide, Quinton wailed and people laughed. Money fell into the hat. Percy joined Monk and side by side they moved in unison, clippity-tap-clippity-clap. Quinton howled again and stepped forward to drop a five-dollar bill in the hat. He'd get it back later. It was seed money to get the folks going.

Sidle-slide, leg slap, chest thump, hip bump, Monk dropped back and blew chords on the harmonica. Percy did his stuff. He was smooth and fluid, a polished professional. Tap-a-dap, slap his heel, tap-a-dap, Quinton Toussaint squealed; tap-a-dap, and now Monk took over. His best moves were really the easy ones, but crowds liked them. He twisted his mouth to show concentration, feet flying, taps singing; Percy on the mouth harp hit every other note, a-one-and-two, and-a-one-and-two.

Suddenly, Monk twirled, flashed a grin and looked at the spectators one after another; they smiled and laughed.

Clickety-clack; slap his back, slap and clap, clickety-clack.

Quinton whooped.

People applauded.

The winds rose up and up.

I HAVEN'T STOPPED DANCING YET

by Greg Herren

War is not hell. Adolescence is. It's a minefield of judgments, dramas, and shunnings. Ask any adult willing to revisit those angsty years and risk a PTSD relapse and you will learn that even the "popular" kids, those charmed ones, experienced self-conscious uncertainty and hidden fears. And if *they* felt the sting of pimply ridicule, then how did the subsets of hangers-on, shut-out observers, and flat-out loners make it through the night? Prayers? Sorcery? Self-immolation?

In my case, in Sunbeam white bread America—rural Kansas in the 1970s—it was similar to Dante's *Inferno*. On steroids. It's kind of like that when you're gay and don't know it, don't have the emotional vocabulary to even feel it. If you think this is going to be the ranting or whining of yesteryear's wannabe, you would be wrong. Because I *was* popular. I had enough testosterone to pass stereotype, even enough to live in jock world and play on the high school football team. I played both ways—right guard on offense and left tackle on defense. In fact, I was living the small-town American dream, outfitted in helmet, shoulder pads, knee pads, cleats—the armor of a gridiron gladiator, knocking other guys down for glory. But back in the locker room, showering, toweling down, cutting up with my teammates, I still wore the armor. I couldn't let my guard down, and I didn't understand why. I even wore the armor, metaphorically, into the classrooms, where I never felt truly comfortable, and down the hallways, where I played the role of a carefree student. I wore it with my family and my friends, at my church, everywhere. Because something was "off." I somehow couldn't even fit in with myself.

But there was one place where I could let loose. At my high school dances, it was out there on the gym floor that I was able to find some kind of joy, shedding my shoes, dancing like a madman in my socks, and losing myself in the music. I felt like I belonged there on the floor, celebrating, throwing off inhibitions. I didn't know what I was expressing, but shaking off all that heavy emotional armor was liberating, physically and mentally.

Sunday Tea Dance in the Quarter is like that for me. It's my favorite night to go out—even if it sometimes means being blurry and tired all day on Monday. There's just a different atmosphere prevalent on Sundays than on the previous nights of the weekend. For one thing, since everyone has to work on Monday, the evening starts earlier. A discerning gay man would *never* be caught dead going out earlier than 11:00 p.m. on a Friday or Saturday night. I like to head out around six on Sundays, find a place to park, and then stroll down Bourbon Street to the Fruit Loop.

The music is always the same—it's trash disco—which makes it even more fun. And there's a sense of tradition about Tea Dance. They always play this hilarious video of scenes from *Mommie Dearest* over a recording of "Mamma Mia" by ABBA. They show the famous clip of "The Night the Lights Went out in Georgia" speech from *Designing Women*, the one where Julia Sugarbaker tells off the reigning Miss Georgia: "Just so you know, Marjorie, and your children *will* someday know, my sister was not just any Miss Georgia, she was THE Miss Georgia," and everyone recites it right along with Dixie Carter. How can you not smile, how can you not relax, in such an environment?

And then of course there's the napkin toss. As the song "Love is in the Air" plays, all the patrons grab a handful of napkins, and on the title line of the song, everyone just lets loose with their napkins. I always aim for the ceiling fans with mine. And whenever I hear the opening strains of that hoary old classic, "It's Raining Men," I instantly transform into over-the-top dance-floor guy. It's magic. As my friend Johnny says, "Greg is the only person I know who can go from zero to drag in five seconds."

That was not always the case, of course. After struggling with my sexual orientation throughout my twenties, I came out at thirty. It should have been totally liberating, like my high school dance floor, but it wasn't. I was living in Tampa, Florida, at the time, a place that felt sterile and unbending. My family back in Kansas disowned me, of course, cut me off, denying me the kind of unconditional love that is everyone's hope. I dated, but no real relationship ever developed, and by the age of thirty-two I gave up, deciding I would probably remain single for the rest of my life. Maybe for those reasons I just couldn't dance. Not with abandon. Not yet. I mostly stayed home, read books, watched television—a misfit, uncomfortable in my skin, wanting desperately to belong—somewhere. Even when I did manage to make it to the bars in Tampa, I would stand on the sidelines and watch, terrified to join the crowd—and if I ever got up the courage to go out there, I was self-conscious and awkward, afraid people were looking at me and laughing. But it was different in New Orleans.

I remember the exact date I fell in love with New Orleans. It was my thirty-third birthday: August 20th 1994. I'd been there before, but I didn't truly experience the city, didn't hear its heartbeat, until that date. I'd always found the place fascinating; I loved reading about it in books like *The Witching Hour* by Anne Rice and *New Orleans Mourning* by Julie Smith. Yet on every previous trip it seemed as though I had somehow landed on another planet. It was dirty, it smelled funny, and Lord, was it hot. It was like every other place to me: alien and foreign, and I was unwelcome.

But this time the city was full of an embracing vibe I had not noticed before, and I could feel it as I walked along the cracked and broken sidewalks of the French Quarter, staring up at the evening clouds stained pink by the reflected neon of Bourbon Street. Maybe my spirit was willing it, needing the rebirth, but the place was also creating a space for it. *You belong here*, the city seemed to be whispering in the dulcet tones of a practiced seductress: *Join me and all of your dreams will come true.* That quiet whispering inside my head wouldn't stop. And as I spent that weekend wandering the peaceful streets of the Garden District, riding the streetcar, and partying all night long in the gay bars, it kept up its steady patter.

And I danced.

The boys in the New Orleans bars were friendlier and more welcoming than I had ever experienced before in any other city. I felt I might be truly part of something on the dance floor. And a few weeks later, when I returned, that feeling was still there, even stronger, that second trip only serving to reinforce it. And I started coming out of my shell. I went back to Tampa with a new mission in life; I was inspired for the first time in years. My dream had always been to become a writer, and while from time to time I would make a stab at it, I would eventually get discouraged and give up again. But New Orleans had whispered to me of possibilities, possibilities that this time seemed real.

I spent the next few months making over my life. I went to work and came home every night and wrote. I stopped watching *All My Children* and *General Hospital* and the endless stream of prime time shows. Instead, I sat down at my word processor and wrote. Even if it was just an angry diary entry about some asshole passenger who'd pissed me off at the airport ticket counter where I worked, I was determined to write, determined to morph into a creative being with something to say. I would hole up in my room, light a cigarette, turn the machine on, and start typing. And every morning when I woke up, I would put in my *Abs of Steel* tape and do that routine plus one hundred push-ups. No more overweight wallflower, no more loser ticket-counter agent. I stopped eating fast food and made healthier choices. I gave up soda. And weight started dropping off of me. My waist was shrinking and my confidence was growing. *If I can keep this up till New Year's*, I told myself every day, *I will join a gym.* And always in the back of my mind was the thought: *And as soon as I can, I will move to New Orleans.*

Meanwhile, I visited the city again on Halloween for the Lazarus Ball, a huge costume party to raise money for Project Lazarus, an AIDS hospice. The Lazarus Weekend is a big Halloween circuit party, really—and it was my first experience with such a thing. I was going as an Egyptian and drove all over Tampa looking for the proper materials for my costume, right down to the royal headdress and sandals with elaborate leatherworking. I was very excited about the weekend, mainly because I was going to get to dance again. And that felt good.

I danced every night that weekend until dawn. I met wonderful, friendly guys from all over the country—and beautiful and muscular as they were, they were nice to me. I felt more and more like I was part of a community for the first time since I'd come out. It struck me that the happiest moments of my life had all occurred over a period of two months—in this Louisiana city. I was flirted with when I returned for New Year's, and I met so many people I couldn't remember them all. During Mardi Gras I went to parades, caught beads, and felt the joy of celebration. But not the kind of joy that was to come when a mutual friend, Lisa, introduced me to Paul Willis. "You remind me of him," she had said many times.

I had been going to the gym obsessively, but despite the almost constant sex I was having, none of those guys were interested in me as a person. I was a body, an object of desire, which ironically left me feeling empty and alone. I had gone from being nonexistent in the gay bars to being noticed, but it was almost worse this way. At least before, I could blame my inability to make friends or to find a lover on my appearance. Now that excuse was gone. Maybe I was just a loser after all.

Paul lived in Minnesota, was going through a bad time, and didn't have any gay friends he felt he could talk to about everything. "I immediately thought of you," Lisa said. "Do you mind if I give him your address and phone number?"

A few weeks later a package arrived for me from Minneapolis. I opened it with some wonder, having completely forgotten my conversation with Lisa. In it was a mix tape, a CD of Sade's greatest hits, a couple of books, and a letter. The letter was five pages long, and he had obviously poured his heart into it. As I read, I began to get a little uncomfortable with this deep, introspective look into the life of a complete stranger, yet at the same time I felt as though he were talking about my life; I could so completely identify with the emotions and experiences he'd had. And, as our correspondence grew, I was amazed at what a warm and funny person this stranger was. We decided to meet at Lisa's apartment in the French Quarter in July.

Many people think the French Quarter is tacky, a blight, an embarrassment to a modern city, with its strip joints, sex clubs, and gay bars. But those are the people who don't truly know the Quarter. After going on twenty years in New Orleans, I still marvel every single time I walk its uneven streets and sidewalks. The Quarter is the grace and loveliness of the Ursulines convent, the magnificence of the Beauregard-Keyes mansion, the smell of grease from the Clover Grill, the Lucky Dog vendors with their huge hot-dog-shaped carts, a Pimm's Cup at the Napoleon House, and the ringing bells of Saint Louis Cathedral. It is also, with its one-way streets, lack of parking, and bizarre street cleaning schedule, a neighborhood, where everyone knows everyone, greeting one another as they carry their groceries home from Matassa's or the A&P on Royal Street. It is courtyards with elephant ferns and fountains, wrought iron lace on the balconies, and the big "UNEEDA BISCUIT" sign on the side of a brick building on Dumaine Street that always makes me smile when I stand on the balcony at Café Lafitte in Exile.

I was paying the cabdriver and lifting my bag out of the trunk when I noticed a man walking up the sidewalk carrying a plastic bag filled with bottles of Diet Pepsi and packs of cigarettes. He was cute, and he had a huge grin on his face. "Greg?" he asked.

I nodded.

His face split into the most beautiful smile I'd ever seen. By that evening, sitting on the balcony at Embers Steak House on Bourbon Street, I was in love. Fortunately for me, he was too. We moved to New Orleans together the next month. But *un*fortunately for both of us, our beautiful apartment, with its twelve-hundred square feet, hardwood floors, ten foot windows and eighteen foot ceilings, was in what was then a rather bad neighborhood. The beautiful park across the street was a hangout for crack heads at night. We could hear them doing business out there, cars slowing down and idling at the curb. Sometimes we could hear people screaming at each other; other times, we heard gunshots. It was 1996, after all, the same year the city was dubbed the "murder capital" of the country.

New Orleans has always been a haunted city, haunted by a long history of slavery and death, Jim Crow, yellow fever epidemics, voodoo and poverty. I sensed that the city and its ghosts were testing us, testing our resolve. And that resolve has damn sure withstood all the tests, including a vicious, brutal hate crime that broke Paul's cheekbone and took out his right eye, a wrongheaded but temporary move to Washington, D.C., and a low down dirty bitch named Katrina. Still, we kept coming back.

Ghosts may walk the streets here, but they are a part of the magic, the mystery, and the charm of our city.

On my very first Sunday back in New Orleans, having been evacuated that August 28th with Katrina on our doorstep, through September and into October, I went to Tea Dance again. And while it wasn't quite the same, I saw some of the old faces I had always seen. And when the napkins flew, my soul soared with them. So what if there were only about twenty people there, as opposed to the mobs that used to crowd around the venerable old bar? There, on the corner of Bourbon and Dumaine, the music was the same and the old spirit was still there.

Paul and I have enjoyed our life together in this city for seventeen years, and look forward to many more. We've had our fortunes told in Jackson Square, and drinks at Galatoire's. We've stuffed ourselves with more shrimp po' boys than we care to remember. We immerse ourselves in the literary life of the Tennessee Williams Festival and the LGBT Saints and Sinners Festival. I was fortunate to get to know my hero, author Julie Smith, who has become my mentor and friend. Her tutelage and advice were instrumental in launching my literary career in 1999. Not even Prince had to tell me how to party that year. Since then, I've written hundreds of thousands of words, and ninety-eight percent of them have something to do with The Big Easy. Which it isn't. Easy, that is.

No, this is not an easy place to live. It never was. "The Big Easy" is not a nickname a local came up with—it was actually coined by musicians because it was easy to find work here—and no locals use the term. But we put up with the difficulties—the ineptitude and corruption, the crime, the usual stupidity—because there is simply nowhere else for those of us who have heard the song of the siren. New Orleans has also been called "Sodom on the Bayou," but we are not ashamed of that designation. We like being able to buy a drink at any time, day or night. We like being able to buy hard liquor at the grocery store or the drugstore. In one of my books I wrote, "A social drinker in New Orleans would be in rehab anywhere else." We make jokes about our relaxed attitude, would never raise our eyebrows or look down our noses with disdain at anyone who had too much to drink. And, in spite of the judgment of those who say Hurricane Katrina was God's punishment for Southern decadence, the Labor Day gay pride celebration that has gone international, well, it seems that many winds are shifting lately. A hurricane of change is bearing down on the old guard, bless their frightened little hearts. More and more young LGBT people are coming out; fewer are taking their own lives. And, as the power of education takes hold, their friends and families are more receptive by the week. The rainbow flags are flying proudly down at the Fruit Loop, with the blessings of the true believers out there, not the faux Christians who refuse to see who we are.

It was a struggle, but the kid who couldn't understand himself now has a clear vision of who he is: a successful writer, a partner to Paul, a friend, a lover of laughter. For years, I was the wallflower at this prom called Life. It was New Orleans that finally dragged me out onto the floor, all fit and muscle-shirted in my cross-trainers. She beckoned to me, crooking her finger and winking, and I followed her out under the disco ball and laser lights, and began to move my feet to her rhythm. And I haven't stopped dancing yet.

SHORT DAYS, DOG DAYS
by Marlin Barton

I don't care what people read in the paper, I never did call it a flying saucer. And I ain't calling it one now. People are saying I've lost my mind, what there was left of it to lose. That's their joke on me. I know. My wife's told me. Sometimes I think I'm her joke. And my lesbian daughter's.

The thing never did make any noise. All I heard was my dogs, Larry and Jack, barking. They made such a racket that I went out with my shotgun and a flashlight. First I thought it might be a possum or a coon walking around the pen, teasing the dogs. They'll do that sometimes. But both Larry and Jack were looking up and baying like they had something treed in that one big water oak that grows in their yard. The thing is, that didn't make sense. The only way anything could get treed in there was to break *into* the pen. I looked up and shined my light anyway.

That's when I saw it hovering. It was kind of glowing, but hardly putting out any light at all. I can't tell you how big it was exactly. Maybe a hundred feet across, and round. No wings on it, none that I could see. It just sat there, or maybe it was spinning. I felt like I was being watched, me and the dogs. Then it dropped, fast, was probably fifty feet off the ground. Larry and Jack really went at it then, not baying like when they tree something, but like when another dog wants to fight. They didn't let up, and I swear the glowing got brighter and maybe it dropped lower and spun faster, because suddenly the air was twisting all around me. That's when I shot at it. First one barrel, then the other one, double-ought buckshot.

The strange thing is, I never heard the buckshot hit anything. I might as well have been shooting at stars. And the next thing I knew, that's what I was looking at. It was gone. I don't mean it flew away. The thing disappeared so fast I didn't even see it disappear.

I stood there a few minutes, not moving, just looking up with my mouth probably hanging open. The dogs got quiet then, settled down in front of their house like nothing had happened. I guess it's all the same to them, a coon or a fox, a strange dog, some machine hovering over them. Once it's gone, they can put it out of their minds and go back to licking themselves.

Things didn't work out quite like that for me.

When I walked back inside Lois was sitting on the sofa in the den, her housecoat closed up around her. "What was you shooting at?" she said. Sounded like she said it just to say something that wasn't part of the argument we'd been having before the dogs interrupted.

Maybe I was still so confused that I didn't think. Instead of mumbling something about a coon, I told her what I'd seen. That thing must have taken my brain with it.

"You're not very funny," she said. Sounded like the argument was creeping back into her voice.

"I'm not trying to be funny."

She quit picking at the button on her housecoat. "You're seriously wanting me to believe you saw a flying saucer?"

"I saw *something*. I swear."

"And shot at it?

"You heard the gun," I said.

"Maybe you shot just to be shooting."

"Why would I do that?"

"You're so sick of arguing that you're making up crazy shit to shut me up."

"Now there's an idea," I said. "I'll have to remember that. Of course it doesn't seem to be working too good right now. *Not* that I'm making this up, even if it does sound like crazy shit to you."

"What else could it sound like? And if there are flying saucers, why would one fly over the dog pen?"

She stared at me a minute and shook her head. Then she got up and walked to the kitchen in those ratty blue slippers that matched her ratty blue housecoat. Looked like she had something in her mind, or up her sleeve. So I followed her. The land line sits on the kitchen table, and she reached and pulled the book out from under it, took a seat and started flipping pages.

"Who are you gon' call?"

"The sheriff, that's who."

"No you ain't neither."

"He lives just down the road, so it won't take him long to get here. He needs to know we're being invaded."

"Put the phone down."

She started dialing, figuring to call my bluff, I guess. I reached over and jabbed my finger onto the cut-off button.

"What are you doing?" she said. "Don't you know this is too important a thing not to call the authorities? They'll want to bring in scientists and government officials. Of course, it'll all be top secret. Now, did you get taken aboard by spacemen? 'Cause if you did doctors might want to take your brain out and study it. Or maybe your brain is already missing and those little green men used your empty head as a slop jar."

I wanted to jerk the phone out of her hand, and if she'd kept on I might have.

"Just admit to me that you didn't see no damn flying saucer out there and I'll hang up," she said.

"I'm sorry, but I saw something hovering over the dog pen," I said. "I'm not lying, and I ain't crazy, and I don't want nobody to know my business." I was about yelling.

What she did next surprised me. She actually hung up the phone. Then she marched into the bedroom. I didn't think she'd give up that easy.

"Quit following me," she said when I came after her. "I'm too tired to keep doing this tonight. I've had enough."

I should have known that was a lie.

We'd been arguing earlier about moving into town. She wanted to. I didn't. This wasn't nothing new. She'd been pushing for it two years. First she said it would be better for Margaret, our daughter, who was still in high school. Said she'd be closer to her friends, would make it easier for her to go places with them. What she really meant was that she wouldn't have to drive Margaret into Demarville all the time, or let Margaret use her car.

All this was before Margaret turned into a lesbian. Lois says I make it sound like Margaret's a monster when I say that. Like I might as well go around telling people that she *turned into* a werewolf, when I'm really the one who turned into a monster, according to Lois.

After I told her moving into town for Margaret wasn't a good enough reason, she started talking about how everybody else around here was already moving. And she was right about that. Boys I grew up with, the ones I thought would never leave, like Carter Finley and Willie Green and Bobby Turner, they're gone, raising their kids in town, living in big brick houses. Some people here when I was coming up you just knew would move off, way off, when they got grown. I say *they* never counted.

And so many of the ones who hadn't moved off are in the graveyard now. I'm only forty-five years old and it seems like I know more dead people than live ones. And the dead ones were better people by a damn sight, like old Mr. Anderson who owned the store by the post office. He was honest as the day was long. The way I see it, we ain't got nothing but short days now. His old store just sits empty, with weeds and bush-es growing up all around it. Only stores left around here are out on the highway, and if you want more than cigarettes, beer, or gas, you better go to town, 'cause you ain't gon' find it here.

So then Lois said, "What about the crack heads and meth freaks?" And she was right. There're some out here now, blacks and whites both. Blacks on crack, rednecks on meth, and some of them homegrown too, making it in trailers that sit on land their granddaddies used to farm and sweat over. But I told her, "They got all that in town too. You can't get away from it." Besides, I ain't letting dopeheads run me off. Some good people got to stay.

Lois shook me awake. "The sheriff's at the door," she said.

Took me a minute to figure out, or remember, what was going on. "Dammit, I can't believe you called him."

"I didn't. I swear." She pulled her housecoat tight around her again, like she was cold, or telling a stone cold lie.

"If you didn't call, why's he here?"

"Maybe somebody heard the shots."

I pulled on some jeans and a shirt as fast as I could. "People who live in the country don't call the law just because they hear a gun go off."

"They might with things the way they are out here these days."

"Bullshit," I said, which turned out to be a mistake.

It was the sheriff at the door, sure enough. He stood there in full uniform with his hat in his hand. "We got a call about shots being fired," he said.

His name was Cook. He was only the second black sheriff we've ever had, but the white people had got used to him, and liked him. I noticed he didn't say why it took him so long to get here, or who had called.

"There was maybe just some animal around my dog pen," I said. "I wanted to run off whatever it was."

"You think it could have been some*body*?"

I was trying to decide if I ought to tell him to come on in, so I didn't answer quick as I should have.

"It might have been little green men," Lois said. She'd slipped up behind me. Now she poked her finger into my back real hard. "Don't tell me *bullshit*," she whispered.

The sheriff looked like he didn't know if we were drunk, stoned, crazy, or having a domestic dispute, which I've heard can be pretty dangerous for a cop.

"He says he saw a flying saucer."

"That ain't what I said." I might have been looking at the sheriff, but it wasn't him I was talking to.

"What exactly did you see?" he asked me then, real calm, like this was a regular kind of thing for people to report.

There wasn't any way out of it, so I described the thing as best I could.

"Let's go take a look around your dog pen," he said.

I didn't see much point in it, but we walked on through the house. I picked up my flashlight. He took his off his belt.

"I know you've never heard anything this crazy," I said once we got outside.

He laughed a little. "You got no idea."

When we walked into the pen, the dogs nosed around him some. There wasn't really anything for him to see. At least I didn't think so at first. But I spotted where some old leaves had been blown around in a way that didn't look natural. I didn't say anything. I only wanted him to go. For all he knew, the dogs had been digging in the leaves.

He shined his light up at me, not right in my face, but close enough where I didn't like it too much. "Why'd you shoot at it?" he said.

I didn't want to say, "Because it scared the shit out of me." So I told him how it had been upsetting Larry and Jack.

He dropped his beam. "No law against shooting a gun out in the country."

"Let me ask you something," I said. "My wife call you?"

He raised his light back up, on my face this time. "Like I said, somebody called in shots being fired. Would have been here sooner, but I was out on the road up north of Valhia." He finally lowered his light a little. "You got a daughter, don't you?"

Now I put my light on him, almost in his face. "Yeah."

"She home? She see anything?"

"No, she moved into town, Demarville, about six months ago."

I thought I saw him smile a little, like he just remembered something funny.

When I got home Thursday afternoon from working at the fertilizer plant, there my daughter sat in the living room with my wife. The weekly paper out of Valhia was spread across the coffee table in front of them.

"Hey, Daddy," Margaret said, like I wasn't about to step into a number two steel trap. Her brown hair looked like she'd just got it cut at a men's barbershop by a drunk barber. It used to be long and full—like her mama's.

Lois started reading from the paper, running her finger across the words. "When Mr. Miller was asked why he shot at the flying object, he responded, 'It was worrying my dogs.'" Her and Margaret started laughing hard. They'd probably been laughing all afternoon. "*Hit was worryin' my dawgs*. I can hear you now," Lois said.

I stood there a minute, like I did after that thing had disappeared back behind the stars, not hardly believing it was all in the paper for everybody to see. My legs felt weak, my stomach too. But the worst of it was them laughing, especially my daughter, who used to think her daddy was the greatest man in the world. Now men in general, and maybe me in particular, don't count for much in whatever world she lives in.

They finally calmed down, but something hit me then that hurt worst of all. "I guess you called the paper and told them all about it," I said to Lois. "Every little detail. You must have been at the back door listening that night."

"I didn't tell the paper nothing," she said.

"Just like you didn't call the sheriff?"

"I didn't do that either. I told you."

Margaret stood up. She was always a little on the stocky side, but looked like she'd lost a few pounds since she moved out, which kind of worried me in a way, strange as that may sound. She propped a foot on the table and leaned toward me. I could see the tattoo on her arm that says *Blah! Blah! Blah!* which I guess is supposed to be all the men of the world talking. First time I saw it, I told her it made her look like a convict at Kilby, the men's prison. That's when Lois said I was a monster. I know I sounded like a jackass, but a jackass only eats hay. They don't spit fire and leave dead bodies in their trail.

"I asked Mama, and she told me she didn't call the paper or the sheriff. She wouldn't lie to me."

"Wish I could believe it, but how else would the paper have known?"

"They look at the police and sheriff's reports every week, Daddy. You know good and well they always list in the paper everybody that's been arrested, and what they've done."

I couldn't believe she'd thrown that up at me. Years back, they listed me in there for theft, stealing a calf, but all I'd done was hold it ransom—until the man's sorry-ass son brought my daughter's bike back that he'd stole out of our front yard. What he wanted with a girl's bike I don't know.

They had me in there for mayhem once, too. But I did not eat that man's dog. If I'd only kept my mouth shut, but that's a whole other story.

"I didn't get arrested, though," I said. "Not this time."

"You're not listening."

I sat down in a chair and pulled my boots off, wondering how many times I'd heard that. I saw the television was on one of those afternoon talk shows, the kind where somebody comes on and talks about their face lift or their combination boob job and penis enlargement and how much better their life is now and everybody applauds. Then they talk about how they wouldn't have ever had that drug problem that almost killed them if they'd only gotten their sex-change operation a little sooner.

"So did you come over to hear your mama read that article to me?" I said.

"No, Daddy. Mama told me about what happened, but I didn't know about the article. Is it so hard for you to believe that I just wanted to come home?" She glanced at her mama real quick, and as soon as their eyes met I knew something was going on.

"Are you planning on staying for supper? You hadn't in a long while," I said.

"I can't. I got some things to take care of."

"Like go out and tell all your friends how your daddy shoots at spaceships that worry his *dawgs*?"

"No, now that it's in the paper, I won't have to," she said, or mumbled really.

Her mother laughed again.

"I guess you been burning up the phone lines," I said to Lois.

"I might have made a few calls since the other night, and a certain subject might have come up. 'Course the phone's rung a few times today since the paper's come out. You're a celebrity."

I looked at the television screen. A man and a woman were slapping at each other and a big guy was pulling them apart. "Yeah, I'm what everybody wants to be," I said.

After supper I fed Larry and Jack and was sitting on the back porch watching them eat. Lois came out and sat beside me. She stared at the woods awhile without saying much. Then I asked her what Margaret had come over for.

"I figured we'd come around to that sometime tonight," she said. "I was just waiting till you were ready."

"So what's going on?"

She looked at me like I was some cripple in a wheelchair. "She's got her a girl that's moved in with her, and I ain't talking about just a room-mate."

I watched Jack jump onto the roof of the doghouse. He likes to stand up there. Larry started barking at him, wanting him to get down 'cause he can't jump up.

"I didn't think about something like this happening. Not yet, any-way."

"Why not?"

"She's too young. And it ain't even been a year since she told us the way she is."

"You mean since she *turned into* a lesbian?"

"That ain't what I said."

"You been knowing just as long as me that she's the *way she is*, and that's been way more than a year."

"No I hadn't either. I've told you that. I didn't know until you sat me out here and told me."

"Bullshit, Miller. You ain't as stupid as you sound."

"Hell, she had dates with boys."

"Which didn't mean much."

I didn't say anything for a minute, just watched the dogs. "Where'd she meet her?" I said finally.

"At the beauty school. The girl's mother owns it."

"Great. Ain't they from California?"

"Yeah. And I got something else to tell you."

"What now?"

"Margaret wants to bring her out here for supper one night."

"No way. I can't have that. That's too much for me. I mean it, Lois. You better hear me."

"Guess you don't want to see this, then." Before I knew what she was doing she reached into her shirt pocket, pulled out a picture, and stuck it in front of me. It was one of Margaret standing in front of a tree with her arm around a tall blond girl, real tan, that you'd never guess in a million years was that way. She could have been a model.

"Looks like Butch and Sundance," I said. "They gon' start them a gang?"

Lois stood up and leaned over me. "You're a shit, Miller. Pure and simple."

About midnight was when the dogs started carrying on again, sounding like they had something treed. I hadn't even been asleep, and I grabbed my flashlight and gun, like before.

When I made it to the pen, Larry and Jack were still baying. I looked for the glow first, then waited to see if I could feel the air twisting. I finally shined my light, but there wasn't nothing there. The dogs, though, they kept right on, like something from some other world was up above us, and just because I couldn't see the thing didn't mean it wasn't there. Maybe it was making high-pitched noises that only dogs could hear.

I started to shoot straight up but decided not to waste shells. You can't shoot or fight what you can't see. So I stood beside the dogs with my head thrown back, looking hard as I could, and probably looked like a fool, too, but at least I wasn't barking mad.

Then the dogs stopped, like somebody'd hit them in the throat at the same time. They were still a minute, and Larry went in their house and Jack jumped on top of it again. I walked over and petted him, maybe to calm myself down as much as him.

I didn't want to go back inside. Since I was already in the doghouse with Lois, I decided I'd just sleep outside with the dogs. I could keep watch on them, and on the piece of space above their pen. So I laid out in the hammock at the edge of the yard, hoping the canvas wasn't too rotten to hold.

Sleeping outside's nothing new for me. I call it going to the Green Hotel. I'll take a pack with a little food and a sleeping bag, some matches and a lock-blade knife. If it's hunting season I'll carry my shotgun. Sometimes I'll be gone a couple of days.

Staying in the Green Hotel was what got me my mayhem charge. One night I settled in close to a camphouse on the Tennahpush River that I didn't know was there, and this mix-bred hound must have smelled me. He started to barking and carrying on, and I couldn't sleep. Finally he got real bold and came up so close I could see him. I'd had enough by that time, and I jumped up cussing and hollering so loud my voice echoed back from across the river. I must have sounded like a crazy man, and I know people heard.

Since I was in an agitated state of mind, I did something I wouldn't ordinarily do. I hit the dog with a pinecone, one that was still green. The dog yelped like I'd scalded him and took off toward the river. I don't know where he went from there, but he was *gone*. Next morning a man come looking for him. Sounded like he was some damn lawyer from Birmingham. Wanted to know if I'd seen his dog. He kept looking from me to my fire to my knife and frying pan. I must have looked like the wild-man-in-the-woods, and I could tell he thought I was crazy enough to have done it. So I said, "Maybe I ate him," and picked my teeth with the point of my knife. A few weeks later he found some bones, but by the time everybody figured out they were from a fox, I'd already been charged. Lois and Margaret were so proud.

I found the man's dog a month later. I named him Larry.

I couldn't sleep in the hammock. Finally, I crept inside, got what I needed, and climbed over our fence. Tore my pants while I was doing it. I walked on into the woods, and about one o'clock in the morning found a high spot, built a fire, and settled in. Since I didn't have to work the next day, I could stay as long as I wanted. I watched the stars and tried not to think about wives who turn on you, or daughters who turn away from you.

By the time I got home the next afternoon, Lois had pulled her own disappearing act. The note she left was on the kitchen table. *You run off again you son of a bitch.*

I knew I'd messed up, but not how bad. I wasn't sure what to do, so to pass the time I gave the dogs a bath and dipped them for fleas. I felt guilty about it later. Figured Lois would say I cared more about the dogs than her or my daughter.

I ate supper alone, and slept in the bed the same way, or tried to sleep, that is. Never did hear her car pull in or the door open. The dogs were quiet too, all night.

At work people kept pointing imaginary shotguns in the air and pulling the trigger every time I drove by on my forklift. And at lunch one old boy named Moose who had a long memory asked me if I was eating a dogmeat sandwich. I put up with all that, didn't say much. Mostly I wondered if Lois would be home when I got there. I knew I could call Margaret and find out probably that Lois was with her, but figured that's what Lois wanted.

Sure enough, the house was dead as a graveyard when I got there. I'd have to tough it out at least one more night. Strange thing is, home didn't feel right. It was like strangers had come in and rearranged everything, except it all looked the same, and then set the house down on some street in a town I'd never been in. I was almost afraid to look out a window.

Larry and Jack started up at a quarter after two, baying and carrying on. I almost jerked the covers off and ran out there again, but told myself the hell with it. For all I cared right then the sons of bitches could land, come on in the house, and fix them some dogmeat sandwiches. If Larry and Jack had kept their mouths shut, maybe none of this would have happened.

The next morning, when I walked out back, both dogs were gone. First I looked inside their house just to be sure, but the only thing in there was the hay I'd put in for bedding. Then I checked to see if they'd dug under the fence. But no holes. Nothing. And the gate had been latched when I'd come through. They hadn't slipped out of it. They were just *gone*, disappeared, and I felt sick to my stomach. How much can a man take? I thought. I wondered if that thing had come all the way down to the ground this time and stole Larry and Jack. Maybe the thing was real enough to have done what I was thinking, but trying to get my mind around the notion about stretched it to the snapping point.

Lois could have come and turned the dogs out. I didn't want to think that about her, but I started calling and went to looking for them in the woods. After two hours of not seeing or hearing anything but my own voice, I quit. If they'd found some way out of the pen that I'd missed, or if Lois had let them out, they'd be gone for days, hunting till they dropped. Hounds will do that. I could find them later, like I'd found Larry.

That's what I told myself, anyway.

After work that day I went home to my empty house and just sat—didn't watch television, didn't go outside, didn't hear the Green Hotel calling. Instead of worrying about my dogs, all I could think about was

Lois. I knew she wouldn't have come after me in the woods for anything, but I was going to have to go after her in town if I wanted her back. She might tell me everything I didn't want to hear, but at least I could count on her to do that, all the way down to calling me a shit. Seemed like she was all I could count on. And if she'd let the dogs loose, I could forgive that.

I'd helped Margaret move into town, so I knew where her apartment was. When I got over there that evening and was about to knock on the door, I heard voices. They stopped when my knuckles hit wood. It took a minute, but Margaret opened the door and stood there. I looked past her but didn't see Lois or any blond girl in the living room.

"I'd like to talk to your mama if I can," I said.

"You all right, Daddy?"

Her question took me aback a little. Something in the way she asked made me feel like I must not be. "Well enough," I said. Before I asked if she was going to let me in, she stepped out and closed the door behind her. Then she walked over and leaned against the hood of my truck. I did the same.

"This is the first time you've come over for a visit," she said. "But this isn't really a visit, is it?"

"I guess not," I said and looked away.

"I'd like it if you came by sometime. If you wanted to."

"I'll have to think about that," I said.

The hurt on her face made me feel like a jackass spitting fire, or some other kind of animal that doesn't really live in the world.

"It's nothing to think about, Daddy. You either come or you don't."

I nodded. It was all I could do.

"Mama's not sure yet," she said.

"About what?"

"Going back home, or about you."

"Let me talk to her," I said. "Tell her I said please."

She went inside, and I stood there feeling like the whole world was watching me.

Lois finally came out. Seemed a little like they were tag-teaming me, but I could see why. "What brings you to town?" she said. She stood across the truck from me. "I know how much you hate it here."

175

"You let my dogs out?" I said, except it wasn't what I meant to say at all.

"What?"

"My dogs are gone."

"I'm tired of being accused of things. And hell no I didn't let your dogs out. Maybe you ate them and forgot. You know you ate Larry once. Maybe you ate him again."

I let that pass. I believed her, though, and believed that she hadn't called the sheriff or the paper either one. Maybe it was something in her tone, or it could be that I just needed to believe her, finally, because everything else seemed too damn unbelievable.

"Maybe your spaceship got them."

"I heard it again, or at least heard the dogs barking at it."

"Damn, Miller. The only place that thing flies is inside your head. And the dogs will turn up."

"So have you moved into town permanent, like you been wanting?" I didn't really think she had, but I had to ask.

"I don't know," she said. "I do know I can't stay here much longer. I'm crowding them." I almost rolled my eyes, and she must have expected me to. "Leave it alone, Miller. She does got her own life."

"And you?"

"My life's been with you for a lot of years. Like I said, I don't know."

"What do I need to do?"

"That's for you to figure out."

I wanted to cuss. But I didn't use any bad language, or ask any more questions. I don't think she expected me to be that smart. She kept looking at me like she was afraid something stupid was about to come out of my mouth. Sometimes all you can do with a woman is not say anything.

"I've got to go back inside," she said. "I'm fixing them some supper."

"The girl in there?"

"Her name's Cameron. And no, she ain't. She'll be home after a while."

"You like her all right?"

"Yeah, I like her all right. But mostly I love our daughter."

The dogs stayed gone that night, and the house felt even stranger than before, like all the clocks were telling a different time and the crazy people on television were about to climb through the screen and start talking to me in my dreams.

Early the next evening, Margaret came pulling up to the house. I'd called, said I'd fry some catfish in the big pot outside. I didn't say anything about her mama, and she didn't either. 'Course I hoped it would make Lois happy that I'd asked Margaret over, but that ain't why I did it.

Margaret stopped the car, and the setting sun glinted strong off the windshield. She opened her door and walked around to the passenger side. I figured she'd brought some food. When the blond girl, Cameron, got out, it was everything I could do to keep from shaking my head and closing my eyes. Margaret was looking, probably expecting that from me. Maybe that's what kept me from doing it. Then Margaret took the girl by the hand. She's got guts like her mama, I thought.

I walked toward them. Way off in the woods, I heard a dog bark.

EAT, DRINK, REPEAT:

One Woman's (Three-Day) Search for Everything

by Susan Cushman

Tuesday morning, 7:30 a.m. Paul Newman's Special Blend Organic Decaf K-Cup goes into the Keurig brewer. Eight ounces of steaming java flow into the white mug with the blue logo from Square Books in Oxford, Mississippi, on one side, and a quote from *Winnie the Pooh Goes Visiting* on the other. Remember the scene where Pooh ate too much and got stuck in the hole in the tree, so he asked Christopher Robin to comfort him? *Then would you read a Sustaining Book, such as would help and comfort a Wedged Bear in Great Tightness?* Breathing in the full-bodied aroma from the handpicked Arabica beans, I stir in three packets of raw sugar until they completely dissolve and then add a quick pour of Land O'Lakes fat free half-and-half. Seventy calories and zero grams of fat. Not as sustaining as a Caramel Macchiato from Starbucks, which I gave up after discovering that each grande Caramel Macchiato (*without* whipped cream) has 240 calories and 7 grams of fat. With whip? Add another 5 to 11 grams of fat.

8:30 a.m. Frosted Cheerios make a sound like an old-fashioned bicycle bell as they tumble into a cornflower blue ceramic bowl with a terra-cotta glaze on the inside. A few ounces of fat-free milk moisten the tiny donuts just enough to set the sugar-coating free but not enough to subdue the crunch each bite delivers, temporarily satisfying the craving triggered by a life-long eating disorder known as *pica*. (Crunching on these cholesterol-fighting nuggets is certainly preferable to ice—which ruins teeth—and clay and other non-food items, long buried in my past.) The method of delivery is an eighteen-gauge Towle Beaded Antique oval soupspoon, which has a nice heft, even when only filled with cereal. After licking the last drops of sugary-sweet milk from the glossy mirrored bowl of the spoon, I am greeted by my image in reverse—turned on my head by my first encounter with food this morning, and already thinking about what comes next.

9:30 a.m. Writing, laundry, writing, bills, writing, Facebook, writing, email. Diversionary tactics only keep the cravings at bay for brief intervals. By mid-morning I remember that McDonald's quits serving breakfast at 10:30 a.m. A mere three blocks separate my kitchen from theirs and the sizzling, greasy sausages snuggled into those buttery biscuits. Rule #1: Only eat sausage biscuits on road trips. After ten-thirty those succulent baby sandwiches are replaced by French fries—tossed around in hot, oily baskets with a blizzard of salt covering every surface of each morsel—the fast food that changed a generation of taste buds forever. Rule #2: Never order French fries. Ever. By 10:30 I have managed to keep my body out of the kitchen for an hour, but my mind is anywhere but on the work at hand. Except that today I'm actually writing about food.

10:30 a.m. I've been awake for three hours with no protein or salt. Generously salted scrambled eggs cooked well-done in real butter like an overly bothered omelet satisfies both needs. But the salt makes me thirsty and the protein doesn't act quickly enough for the instant blood sugar boost I'm craving, so I wash them down with a few sips of ice cold canned Coke. I open one can a day and sip on it for about twenty-four hours—my replacement for diet colas, preferring quality to quantity. I was so excited when the new six-ounce cans came out—the ones shaped like tiny little Red Bulls—because of the way they feel in my hand, and they help me cut down on calories. Or at least that's the plan. The edge of the can has an almost sensual feel on my lips as the quintessential caramel-colored thirst-quencher glides down my throat, delivering a refreshing carbonated rush. But as I finish washing the saucepan and putting my dishes away, the craving only grows stronger. *Sugar. Chocolate.* I scoop a couple of dips of Edy's Slow-Churned Rich & Creamy vanilla ice cream—the kind with half the fat, of course—into a stemless martini glass. Next I drizzle Hershey's chocolate syrup over the ice cream, enough to assure chocolate to the last bite. This time a Towle teaspoon delivers the goods, its smaller shape being more efficient at scraping out the final bits of chocolate syrup that cling to the bottom. When the spoon doesn't do the job, I use my tongue. By now the morning is nearly gone. I've achieved very little real work, and shame sets in.

11:30 a.m. How many times do I look at the clock, waiting for permission to pour that first drink? Some days I make it until afternoon. But not today. I realize I haven't stopped eating, drinking, or thinking about eating and drinking all morning. I don't need the bathroom scales to tell me I'm at my all-time heaviest weight. My clothes remind me each time I shed my stretchy yoga pants for jeans or my baggy T-shirt for a fitted blouse. I've put away close to a thousand calories before noon, with plans to prepare a nice oven-roasted pork tenderloin, baked sweet potatoes and fresh Brussels sprouts for dinner. None of those foods appeal to me, but they are favorites of my husband and daughter. I already know that I will sit down to dinner and only nibble at the nutritional fare my body really needs. By seven tonight I'll be full, but still not satisfied. And so at 11:45 this morning I pour a glass of Monkey Bay Sauvignon Blanc into a small pink Depression glass wine goblet I got at an antique store in Arkansas. It doesn't have the same feel as the larger, clear white wine goblets from William Sonoma, but I can't hide them in the dishwasher amongst the coffee mugs and juice glasses like I can the smaller glasses. I save the larger ones for evenings when my husband is imbibing with me. Anticipation builds with the sound of the cork leaving the bottle. The distinctive *chug chug chug* of the wine filling the glass. It's not really a cork—it's a rubber wine stopper (from Rabbit) and its phallic shape and texture is tempting. I place it in my mouth and suck the last drops of wine from its surface as I slowly pull it away and push it back into the bottle. The first swallow is always the best, bringing instant gratification, holding promises of relief, of edges softening, jaws relaxing, mind slowing down, dark clouds abating. And sometimes it makes good on those promises, but the relief is only temporary. Even now as I'm penning these words, the afternoon has begun and a second glass of wine is calling.

12:30 p.m. My husband's perma-press shirts and khaki pants are washed, dried, and hung, wrinkle-free, in his closet—mindless work that somehow soothes because I can be successful in this endeavor. I love the way the Egyptian cotton feels and smells as I rescue his shirts from the dryer. The comfort is short-lived, as my mind returns to food, and to the fact that everything I've eaten today has either been simple carbo-hydrates or protein. Not one of the recommended five daily servings of fruits or vegetables has graced my lips, unless you count wine as a fruit, in which case I'm now on my second serving. I look around the kitchen and find fresh peaches ripening in a small brown bag on the counter. I pull one out and make a small indentation in its flesh with my thumb—it feels ripe. I bring the fuzzy yellow-red orb to my nose (I always smell my food before tasting it) and breathe in its sweet aroma. It's ready. Using a small, white-handled Cutco paring knife, I make one incision, then another, allowing a perfect slice to be removed from the peach. I observe its texture—free of pithiness—and its color: red tendrils, freshly pulled from the seed, contrast with the shiny yellow crescent. I put the entire slice into my mouth and savor it slowly. I give it an 8. If it were a 10, I would eat the rest of the peach naked. Instead, I pour a small amount of white sugar onto a saucer and dip the remaining slices, one at a time, into the sugar before eating them. No longer savoring the flavor, I eat mindlessly, reaching into the bag for another peach, dipping one slice after another into the sugar, waiting for a surge of energy and wonder-ing if it will sustain me for an afternoon of writing and working out and preparing dinner.

1:30 p.m. A second glass of Monkey Bay carries me just past 1,500 words of this essay but the sugar high is over and the salt craving has returned with a vengeance. *Chips.* I want chips with guacamole (that's a fruit, right?) or cheese dip. But if I go there, will I make it upstairs to work out? I hurry to the elliptical, rushing past the pantry and upstairs onto the machine that will help me burn some of those empty calories and hopefully shoot some much-needed endorphins into my nutritionally and chemically unbalanced system. I run down my list of recorded shows on TiVo and settle on last night's new episode of *Law and Order: SVU*, which requires a bit of mental energy to follow. I fast-forward through the commercials, assuring a food-free media session, although it's nearly impossible not to notice the butter dripping off the pasta in the Olive Garden spots, even at double-fast-forward. I actually slow down to watch one of them, nearly drooling into my water bottle in the process.

2:30 p.m. Four and a half hours until dinner. Plenty of time to metabolize a snack first, right? A little queso dip into the microwave and a dozen or so crisp, salty tortilla chips from the pantry join me by the sink where I stand to eat them while watching more of my favorite TiVo-ed shows—this time it's an old episode of *House*. The queso is only "medium" but I don't do hot and spicy so it's burning my mouth just enough to push my margarita button. But I swore off making margaritas at home a long time ago, so I mix up a short Tanqueray and diet tonic with lime. My glass is a wonderful little oval-shaped number from Pottery Barn with wavy lines etched inside. I start with ice—to fill the glass about two-thirds to the top—and then squeeze the fresh lime over the ice, dropping the lime wedge into the glass. The gin comes next. I don't measure, but guess at the shot—1.5 to 2 ounces. The fizzy diet tonic brings it all to life. I can feel the carbonation tickle my nose as I pull the glass to my mouth, smell the lime and finally, the Tanqueray. I celebrate the marriage of chips and queso with gin and tonic for about thirty minutes. And then it's over. I place my hand over my full belly, moving it across my disappearing waistline and running it quickly over my growing love handles. I consider purging, a practice I haven't outgrown from my teenage years. More shame sets in.

3:30 p.m. Two thousand calories in and three drinks under my belt, I face the computer screen and close my eyes. Maybe I need a nap. It's either that or another gin and tonic. I'm in no shape to work. The couch wins, and I allow myself the luxury of reading—not just for pleasure but also as research for my novel-in-progress. I'm fascinated by Michael Cunningham's book, *The Hours*. Lured into the interior worlds of Virginia Woolf, Clarissa Dalloway and '50s housewife Laura Brown for a while, I don't think of food, or drink, or my own insecurities. Until I get to the part where Laura Brown's husband leaves for work and she's left alone with her son and her responsibilities as a mother. "When her husband is here, she can manage it. She can see him seeing her.... Alone with the child, though, she loses direction. She can't always remember how a mother would act." Suddenly I remember that I'm alone, and like Laura Brown, my husband isn't here to see me, to remind me, if only by his presence, how to act. The familiar fog of disgrace creeps back in. I know I should get up and do something productive, but instead I find my way to the freezer for a Skinny Cow ice cream sandwich. Only 140 calories. I take the sandwich back to the couch and continue to read as I taste the cold, low-fat vanilla ice cream wrapped perfectly in the soft chocolate wafers, which stick to my fingers, requiring licking and sucking to get the bits of chocolate off my fingertips. The process distracts me from my reading, and I return to the freezer for another ice cream sandwich. And yes, a third one, tossing the empty container into the trash, burying it beneath the morning's cereal box.

5:30 p.m. Time to start dinner for my husband and daughter. I preheat the oven to 350 degrees for the pork tenderloin. Opening the refrigerator to get out the sprouts and sweet potatoes, I see the limes. Another gin and tonic will ease the discomfort of preparing a dinner that I'm too full to eat. A cocktail before dinner—what could be more benign? My husband and daughter arrive home from work. *Hi, honey, I'm home. Kiss. How was your day? Oh, fine. Mmm, supper smells delicious, what is it? Pork tenderloin, Brussels sprouts and baked sweet potatoes. Aren't you joining us, Mom?* Hug. She grabs a Stella from the fridge and he mixes a Vodka and 7 with lemon. *No, I'm really not hungry, and besides, I kind of snacked all day.* Husband and daughter both smile. *But I'll sit and have a drink and visit with you guys while you eat.* The Brussels sprouts' tiny leaves are bright green and glistening. Brown sugar and butter dissolve into the rich orange flesh of the sweet potatoes. Mustard and honey drip from the skin of the pork tenderloin. Nutritionally and aesthetically balanced. *So what did you do today, dear? I wrote an essay about food.*

8:30 p.m. The evening is filled with talk of our daughter's impending move to Colorado and plans for her wedding next spring. And my trip to Denver in a week to visit our son and meet my new granddaughter, two weeks old. Our daughter is leaving the nest—forever—in two days. So tomorrow afternoon we have appointments for mother-daughter manicures and pedicures at The Nail Bar down in Harbor Town, followed by drinks at Tug's Grill on the Mississippi River. Later we'll meet her dad at our favorite sushi restaurant downtown.

11:30 p.m. My husband sleeps soundly beside me. Our daughter is upstairs. Probably on the phone with her fiancé or watching a movie on her computer. The lonely silence beckons me out of the bedroom. It feels like I'm sleepwalking to the kitchen. I open the refrigerator and find the Monkey Bay from earlier this afternoon. About one-third full. I twist off the top and consider which glass to fill. Fuck that. I put the bottle to my lips, empty it in four swigs, and toss it into the trash. I reach under the cabinet for a new bottle and put it in the refrigerator for tomorrow.

Wednesday morning, 7:30 a.m. My sweet husband brings me coffee in bed, our usual morning routine. I remember as I awaken that today is the day. Our daughter is packing to move. But we have the afternoon at the Nail Bar to look forward to. Then drinks and sushi. The anticipation quells my hunger somewhat. And I'm not alone in the house today. There's someone here to see me, or as much as I am willing to be seen. And so I spend the morning focusing on the delayed gratification of the afternoon and evening, which fills the emptiness. I avoid binging, work out on the elliptical, and make it through four hours without constant thoughts of food and drink. I write a blog post and answer emails, check out Facebook, breathe in and out. Find my way upstairs to the elliptical.

11:30 a.m. After a good workout I begin to feel physical hunger—a sensation I welcome, hoping it means that my metabolism is catching up with yesterday's mother lode of calories. My husband comes home for lunch, my daughter finishes her pre-move errands, and we enjoy a light fare of pita bread, hummus and fresh peaches. I toast the pita with a thin smearing of softened butter, cut it into triangles, and arrange them around the pine nut hummus, which has been dipped into lotus bowls. The cold, smooth olive-oil-topped hummus contrasts perfectly with the buttery pita points. It all washes down smoothly with half a can of Coke. And yes, it would be better with a glass of wine, but we'll be at the bar by four-thirty or five, right? Time to get back to the essay at hand. The next couple of hours are absorbed with writing and occasional interruptions from my daughter as she continues to pack for her move.

1:45 p.m. Time to shower. By this time yesterday I was on my third drink, so what could it hurt to have a small glass of wine while I'm show-

ering and dressing for the afternoon and evening? *Twisted*. That's my
favorite pinot grigio, and the open bottle in the fridge is hard to avoid.
My husband has gone back to work and my daughter is running errands.
Chug chug chug flows the fruity white liquid into a disposable plastic cup—
easier to manage in the bathroom. The first sip of the day is always magical. I carry the cup into the shower with me, but it's gone before I can
rinse the shampoo from my hair, and I dry off quickly, thirsty for a refill.
A second pour accompanies my after-shower routine. By 2:45 I'm ready
to leave for the Nail Bar, with only about 600 calories consumed.

4:30 p.m. Manicures and pedicures are done and we're off to Tug's
Grill. It's still too hot to enjoy the patio so we head straight to the bar.
The top-shelf margarita awakens my cravings as I sip it slowly over the
next thirty minutes while enjoying my last outing with my daughter
before she moves away.

5:15 p.m. We meet my husband at Blue Fin for sushi. He's a few
minutes late, so we get started with a beer for my daughter and a glass
of Ferrari-Carano fume blanc for me. Peppery aromas of lime zest and
lemongrass are complemented by the crisp freshness of grapefruit and a
deeper suggestion of ripe pear. (Okay, I read that on the label, but only
after I picked up on those scents and flavors myself.) After my husband
joins us, we enjoy five different sushi rolls and conversation that's a bit
sentimental and void of very much day-to-day chatter. It is, after all, our
last dinner with our daughter before she moves to Denver to be with her
fiancé. The Lobster Roll is my favorite; the Dragon Roll runs a close second. My daughter compliments my improved skills with the chopsticks
since our last sushi outing and I remind her that it's only one of many
skills she has taught me over the years. I touch each piece of roll lightly
into the soy sauce dish before placing the entire morsel into my mouth.
Crunching down on the festival of flavors and textures in each tiny
masterpiece is like a private party for the taste buds. Eating and drinking
slowly tonight, savoring the moment, I find that I am full before finish-
ing the rolls, and I skip dessert, taking only a taste of my husband's trio
of ice creams when they arrive. I finish the day somewhere under 1,500
calories, and without my usual feelings of bloatedness and guilt. Back
home, I crawl in bed around nine, knowing that I'll be up at five-thirty
to take my daughter to the airport. Around nine-thirty she plops down

on the bed beside me for a "last night at home" chat. When she leaves the room, around ten, my soul—and my belly—are full and I quickly fall asleep.

Thursday, 5:30 a.m. There's only time for one cup of coffee before driving my daughter to the airport. The drive is lovely, with the sun coming up across the expanse of the runways. We don't talk much, but there's a lot of feeling in the air. We hug goodbye, knowing we'll see each other in a couple of weeks when I fly out to visit my son and his family, so the parting doesn't feel like forever. Until I get back into the car and look over my shoulder at this beautiful young woman pulling her suitcases through the glass doors of the airport and out of this phase of our lives, forever. I make it a few blocks away from the airport before turning into a McDonald's for a sausage biscuit—a replacement for the one I managed to avoid on Tuesday. I only eat around the outside of the sandwich, where the biscuit is brown and the sausage is well-cooked, tossing the soggier center bite into the bag. The fountain Coke on ice cools my throat, as I weep most of the way home. By the time I arrive I pull myself together and greet my husband cheerfully.

6:30 a.m. He's getting ready for work, but we briefly discuss our plans for the evening. We're going to the twelfth-annual *Memphis Business Journal's* Health Care Heroes Awards banquet because he is one of the twenty nominees up for five awards. He has been nominated for the "Health Care Heroes in Innovation" award. The other three nominees have sexier platforms (children's cancer treatments and surgical advances, biomedical engineering devices) than his nearly four decades of research in hypertension, so he doesn't expect to win. I'm used to accompanying him to medical meetings. I've been doing it for almost forty years. In May I went with him to Washington, D.C., where he was presented with a national research award. I often eat or drink too much at these events, out of nervousness, anxiety, and feelings of insecurity in the company of so many brilliant and accomplished people. As soon as he leaves for work I begin a familiar cycle.

8:30 a.m. It starts innocuously enough, with a bowl of fresh peaches I cut up the night before. They're a little mushier than they were when I first cut them on Wednesday, and the sugar I sprinkled on them has melted into a syrup, leaving me wanting the texture of the crystals. If not sugar, salt. I recognize the danger signals and hurry away from the kitchen to the computer, replacing the fix with an hour spent on Facebook and email before returning to the essay at hand.

10:30 a.m. I go upstairs into my daughter's empty room, and the tears start up again. I hug her stuffed animals, one at a time—the bears, and especially the blue dolphin—and sit on the edge of her bed. Only a few books remain on her shelves and some remnants of her life with us are still tucked away in her closet. She lived in this room for the past three summers during graduate school, while she worked for an architectural firm in West Memphis, Arkansas. Other than that, it had been nine years since she left us for college and a couple of years of working before grad school. But these three summers were the best times for us as mother and daughter, and now I want to hold those memories close forever. I take her towels downstairs to the laundry room and picture the new life she's moving on to, and I hope that she will find everything she wants in her marriage, her family, and her career. My tears have awakened my hunger and I head into the kitchen.

11:30 a.m. It starts with chips and guacamole—homemade with fresh avocados and tomatoes from the farmer's market, a squirt of lime and salt. I finish the bowl with about a third of a bag of chips, washing them down with Coke. In the background I play some old episodes of *Glee* that I've recorded, mainly listening to the show tunes as I continue my binge. Next up is a grilled-cheese sandwich. First I melt a few tablespoons of real butter in the skillet. I dip a piece of bread in the butter, put it on top of the cheese, and place the sandwich into the butter with the bare side of the bread down. It smells sweet as it sizzles, and I turn it to check the patterns of brown and yellow on the other side. When it's done I cut it on the diagonal and spread sweet pickle relish on top (something I learned from a friend in my Mississippi childhood) and take it with me into the den. I eat it in front of the television, which mutes the enjoyment and numbs my mental alertness.

12:30 p.m. Making another attempt at writing pulls me back into reality and I realize what I've just done. The sadness leads me to the refrigerator for my first glass of wine for the day. I'm back to sauvignon blanc now, and I go through two glasses fairly quickly, bringing my calorie count to around 1,200 by the middle of the day. In a few short hours I'll be dressing up for the awards banquet, sitting nervously by my husband's side, meeting and greeting the other medical professionals and their spouses. Trying on several pairs of shoes before the mirror in our bedroom—like a little girl playing dress-up—I set out the black heels. But I don't feel pretty. After binging all day on chips and grilled cheese and sausage biscuit and wine, the self-hatred drives me to my knees once again. But not in prayer. My reflection in the bottom of the toilet bowl— and a fetid memory long ago encoded in my frontal lobe—are enough to trigger my seasoned gag reflex. This ritual takes less than a minute. I puke up most of what I've eaten in the past couple of hours. It brings relief, but not without more self-loathing. I cannot, as James Baldwin urged, "vomit the anguish up."

2:30 p.m. I need to work out, shower and get ready for the evening. I allow myself half a can of Coke, to quell the after burn from vomiting and to soothe my esophagus and stomach.

6:00 p.m. We arrive halfway through the cocktail reception. I have a gin and tonic, which I carry with me into the banquet at six-thirty. There's been a mix-up in the seating arrangements, and our friends fill a round table for ten, leaving us to sit with one single man at another table, alone, just us three. Feeling embarrassed and left out, I slip back out to the cash bar for another gin and tonic. Anxious to get off my feet—why did I wear these fucking heels?—I return to my seat at our near-empty table. When the food arrives, I nibble at the flattened chicken breast, cold pasta and overcooked vegetables. Even the key lime pie— my favorite dessert—isn't very good, so I leave most of it on the plate as I continue to glance awkwardly at the seven empty places at our table, wondering if the looks I'm receiving from others in the room are ones of sympathetic embarrassment. When the program begins, the twenty nominees' pictures are put up on two screens in the room as each one's bio is read. The crowd—about two hundred and fifty people—stands and applauds as each winner receives his award. When the third award is announced, we hear my husband's name spoken from the platform in the front of the room: "William Cushman." All the eyes in the room are on us as we stand and I kiss him, and he makes his way from our mostly empty table in the back corner to the stage up front. His brief acceptance "speech," handshakes, and photo ops fill the next few minutes, and as he returns to me, a number of our friends at the next table come over with their congratulatory hugs and smiles.

8:30 p.m. On the drive home, we talk about the award and my husband's surprise. He's a humble man who works quietly under the radar, enhancing and saving the lives of millions of people with high blood pressure all over the world on a daily basis. I love him and I'm proud of him, but the evening has been difficult. As we watch the 10 p.m. news (hey—there's Joe Birch, Channel 5 anchor, who was emcee at the awards banquet) the gin and tonics wear off and I pour two fingers of Crown over ice for my husband and two for me. I fight back the tears as I sit in the den with him. My husband's success can't touch the dark recesses of my damaged spirit, but only adds to the clutter of our life's minutiae. As he retreats to the bedroom after the news, I pick up *The Hours* from the coffee table and continue to read.

SHOE BURNING

by Janet Nodar

What will the ashes mean?
Ghosts banished, losses faced? Beginnings?

This is an occasion for telling tales
for watching sparks loft upwards
from a bonfire under a reaching oak
to sizzle in the Spanish moss.

Oh, we are picturesque,
engaged in this deliberate ritual
yet somehow scraped out all the same.

I was fortunately seated at the shoe burning.
The musicians triangulated nearby.
One began to play and then another and another;
people swayed in the firelight, humming the choruses,
tossing their lives into the flames.
Some burned their shoes up angrily.
Some hopefully, discarding the past; some looked
for prophecy in the flames.

A newbie, I had no loafers to spare.
No journey-worn offering.
My knowledge of the fire remained theoretical.

Next year maybe I could give up my plastic sandals.
I bought them in Brooklyn one hot Sunday.
I was hunting anything, anything at all to shod
an unexpectedly naked foot
which turned out to be orange Vera
Wang jellies: $60, on sale. That hurt.
But these are shoes for melting, not
burning. I might need a cauldron.

What about that sweet pair of taupe suede pumps,
ornately stitched? They are so pretty,
but flimsy and capricious to wear.
I have not donned them in a decade
but still they would be hard to see aflame.

What about the black boots I really love?
The ones I wear all winter?
Is this the sort of burning that would matter?
Is this what the gods of fire prefer?

Growing up, I wanted no shoes at all.
I wanted the spring of grass under my feet,
the mist-drenched green of Puget Sound.
That's a long, long walk from here.

I had no fear of fire when I was young.
I did not know that scorching lasted.

I should burn something that has cost me.
Something shameful, something hard.
I should burn a need I can't fulfill.
I should burn some flame that tempts me.
I should burn some pain I can't discard.

❧

Life has curled around itself, deposited me here
amongst the serenaded
beneath an oak, beneath the stars,
beside a southern stream
attending
a burning.

HOLDING ONTO THIS ONE

by Chuck Cannon

I was raised up Southern sentimental — a holder onto — a keeper of things.

I held onto this one shoe, from a pair of little shoes I likely wore no more than a dozen or so times, proving I tend toward hanging onto that which ain't of any apparent use to anybody, me included.

It is the holding onto, I suppose, which renders any importance at all to the multitude of useless things that populate the nooks and crannies of my dresser drawers, old suitcases, and duct-taped-together boxes that probably ought to have been thrown out with the trash of years ago. Only years ago it wasn't of trash, and somehow, some why, someplace deep inside me could not let go.

I held on.

All my holding onto has ended me up with a mess of scattered and random artifacts from my bygone — mementos — each with their own story.

There are keys to doors I used to live behind that won't ever unlock anything again. Tee-shirts from yester-places folded ever away, never worn, but never finding their way into that bag I fill for the Goodwill. Bits of barely readable lyrics scribbled on scraps of paper — whiskey-smeared ink on bar napkins and faded pencil on the backs of hotel envelopes — songs gone and unwritten because the moment of meaning passed into the mystery before the melody ever came singing those words back to me. There's a three-pack of Hanes size 30 tighty-whitey underdrawers, still in the sealed plastic bag they came in, because they were a gift from my Grandaddy that last Christmas he was still with us. Birthday cards, love notes, all my younguns' baby teeth, worn out wallets, movie ticket stubs, along with one slightly scuffed, hardly worn, little white leather baby shoe.

Somehow, I ended up with only the one, from a pair of what were called "first walkers," being as how they were designed for the feet of a child taking his first few upright steps. It is clearly not one of the first shoes Mama put on my feet, as having a baby attached to a foot big enough to fill a shoe of such size would have likely killed her dead, and she was to save her dying for later, after my little sisters and me had just enough time to get good and used to her being Mama.

This lonely little baby shoe is one of the only things I still have from the time in my life that could qualify for what most folks call normal — from the days when it was still of a pair — back in the yonder when Mama's kisses were made of the magic medicine that took all the hurt away, and Daddy had him one of them smiles that made pretty much any and everybody a believer in whatever it was he decided they were supposed to believe. When the fleece on Mary's little lamb was still white as snow, and Jesus loves me this I know, and God His Own Self answered the prayers of the faithful and miraculously cured The Cancer before it took mamas to heaven, leaving broken daddies who couldn't believe in much of anything.

It was less than a year after I was born when my Daddy, just like his Daddy before him, was ordained as a Pentecostal Holiness preacher. He was early in his twenties when The South Carolina Conference of The International Pentecostal Holiness Church assigned him his first church to pastor in the town of North, South Carolina.

I remember us living in a little white house with green shutters up a steep and rutted dirt driveway, where Daddy set bad examples by wearing his undershirt to the breakfast table, which Mama said did not look presentable, and by leaning back on the back legs of his chair, which Mama said I wasn't allowed to do, on account of I might fall over backwards and break my fool neck, and then how would I look?

I took my chances though, and when she was stirring the breakfast grits, or getting Daddy some more coffee, I'd lean back in my chair while holding on to the edge of the table. I'm pretty sure Mama knew. My ever-smiling Daddy knew too — less than an arm's length away, watching, ready to catch me should I fall, and winking us our own little secret.

I think Mama and Daddy knew something else too; they were doing right to allow me my little dance with the danger, so long as I was holding on.

The two years we lived there, Daddy performed all the duties of a pastor while buying, cleaning and selling old cars on the side so to make all the ends meet. He studied all day Saturdays, preached sermons on Sundays and polished bumpers on Mondays. He baptized sinners in the Name of The Father, The Son, and The Holy Ghost and sold them old Fords or Chevrolets, but never a Chrysler because, he explained, he might have to stand before the people he sold 'em to and preach The Gospel. He visited the sick, eulogized the dead, married those in love and dedicated their babies to The Lord, anointing those little heads, hands and feet with olive oil rendered Holy by the Cross painted on the glass-stoppered bottle it was kept in. Sometimes, Daddy would carry the note when somebody needed a car but didn't have the credit down at the Savings and Loan.

Mama headed up the Women's Auxiliary. She made lemon meringue pies for bake sales, taught Sunday School, led the choir, and directed the Christmas and Easter Pageants — so called, as "plays" were deemed sinful by us Pentecostals. She did the grocery shopping, made breakfast, dinner and supper, and tended to me.

One spring night, they left me with Granddaddy and Grandmama and went off to Columbia, only to come home the next day with my little sister Reneé, who was the prettiest baby anybody had ever seen. She was still in her own first walkers when one fall day Mama brought home another girl child, who was the baby angel we called Sherri for the sixteen years the Good Lord saw fit to let us have her.

Not even six Christmases later, the three of us climbed up into the attic of our new house to get the decorations down that very first December we put them up without Mama to show us how.

There, under our broken-antlered Rudolf, lay a box with stenciled golden letters: *Memories Of Our Firstborn Son, Chuck*. Mama made it and filled it with my firsts: a palm sized New Testament and Psalms, a boy-blue bib needle-pointed in cursive with, *God is Great God is Good*. There was a lock of hair bound on one end with Scotch tape, yellowed by the years, still holding fast to a deckle-edged black and white of my impossibly young Daddy, holding up a crying me for my laughing Granddaddy, his barbering shears open, ready to make that first cut. There was a tarnished miniature spoon, putting the lie to the "stainless steel" inscription on its handle.

Safe and secure in that box of memories was a washcloth-sized remnant of dirty white satin — all that was left of the christening blanket Mama swaddled me in on that bright Sunday morning I was dedicated to Jesus, Our Soon-Coming King — the first thing I remember holding onto — the warm and soft security I slept with, woke up with, ate with, and dragged around til it turned into feather-leaking tatters.

And right there, amongst all this treasure, was a pair of baby shoes, last held, and first held onto, by Mama.

I was not yet three years old when Daddy was assigned to pastor the Pentecostal Holiness Church in Myrtle Beach, South Carolina. There, a small congregation of souls, consisting mostly of womenfolk and a fine crop of young'uns not yet big enough to tell their mamas they ain't goin' to church, all gathered together to praise Jesus at least three times a week — twice on Sunday and every Wednesday night for the prayer meeting and testifying service.

The Good Lord knows they rolled holy, making a joyful noise, worshiping the God of Abraham, Isaac and Jacob, in a run-down two-story stucco building out on Highway 501, right there on the right, as you're headed out of Myrtle Beach, going toward Conway.

My Uncle Wesley told me he drove all the way from Florence to Myrtle Beach, after conducting his own Wednesday night service, just so he could help Daddy paint the whole floor of that old church in white oil-based, so it would have time to dry before Daddy's first Sunday service. He said, "Your Daddy wanted to set the tone for his vision of what that little church was to become. It was near daylight by the time we got done paintin' and we was dizzy as coots, just a-laughing our 'A's' off — but

Son, you ain't ever seen such beautiful surprise in the eyes of a fellowship of believers as when they walked onto that newly painted floor for the first Sunday service your Daddy preached there in Myrtle Beach."

Daddy started right off telling everybody he could tell about his miracle-vision for a brand new church, there in Myrtle Beach. It only took him and Mama two months of Sundays to have that little congregation believing right along with them that they could aspire to a more fitting house of worship — with the help, no doubt, of those few faithful women who likely pestered their husbands to no end about coming to church on Sunday morning to hear the handsome new preacher preach down the glory, and to hear his pretty wife, my Mama, sing like an angel on loan from heaven, accidentally and temporarily earthbound.

They were both deadly good-looking and as charming as Jesus. The two of them, babies in tow, spent all their days that fell between Sundays, visiting with and praying for those who were lonely and laid up sick in the hospital.

They joked with and listened to the lies of the slow-talking, fast-thinking, cigarette-smoking deal-makers who paced the used car lots, waiting for somebody who needed a car and had themselves a small down payment. They shook the calloused and greasy hands of the mechanic men who would tune and fill 'er up at the Texaco, where you could trust your car to the man who wore the star.

Mama got the low-down from gossiping, gum-popping, big-haired women who beauticianed at Sherry's Cut and Curl while Daddy hung out with the newspaper-reading men under a blue haze of smoke and talcum powder, waiting their turn for one of the three chairs at Enoch and Ernie's barbershop.

They took mamas and grandmamas to see wayward sons and fathers out at the Horry County Jail, and cried real tears with those sad souls surrounded by the cloying smell of flowers and death over at Goldfinch Funeral Home.

Mama and Daddy loved on those people so much that within the first year that little congregation doubled in attendance to nearly forty strong. Adding in the ever growing crop of kids under twelve years old, there were regularly fifty or sixty souls coming to worship at that little church where, I am sure you can imagine, most all the mamas' babies were sportin' little white leather shoes whilst taking those first few steps along the straight and narrow.

Those beautiful people came to see and believe in Daddy's miracle-vision of a new church — the one he famously illustrated with a ballpoint pen on the inside of a Thom McAn shoe-box lid.

Sunday by Sunday, Mama charted their faithful giving to the building fund on a big piece of white construction cardboard, displayed on the easel by the piano, where she drew a thermometer in black magic marker and outlined it in blue, because plain black is tacky. As the building fund grew, red magic-marker ink filled up the thermometer until that shining Sunday morning it exploded through the green $10,000.00 goal. The rafters rattled with "Glory Hallelujahs," and "Praise the Lords." We had church all day and dinner on the grounds, special singing and all. With ten whole thousand dollars in the building fund, that little congregation, in heartfelt humility, attributed their accomplishment to the miracle-working God they worshiped.

They took that money and bought a few acres way down on the south end of town where, back then, there wasn't much of anything except the Air Force Base, a trailer park, and a real nice graveyard directly across the highway.

Those men and women who believed in and shared the miracle-vision came in the early hours before, and the weary hours after they went to their regular blue and no-collar jobs. With their tractors and their bulldozers, their shovels and their rakes, they cleared the land. Then they brought their hammers, saws and paintbrushes and shed their blood, sweat and tears and built for their own selves a new and beautiful church that rivaled any of the structures they had heretofore been hired to erect for those uptown denominations of Christians there in Myrtle Beach.

They finished it in white brick, symbolizing purity. They fashioned windows in the shape of crosses with stained-plastic panes of purple, representing royalty; blue, calling to mind the sky where heaven is; and gold, reminding them of their riches stored up in Glory. It was carpeted in red, signifying the Cleansing Blood of Christ, The Crucified King.

Just over a year from the groundbreaking ceremony, the last board suffered the saw, the last nail yielded to the hammer and the last coat of paint dried on Myrtle Beach's newest church, standing proud out on

South Highway 17 — the very road the Father of our Country, George Washington his self, traveled while touring our newly formed nation after he whupped the Redcoats' asses for good up in Yorktown.

On his historic tour of our newborn country, General Washington told 'em all, over and over, loud and clear, that seeing as how we just fought a war to rid ourselves of kings and such, he wasn't about to be called king. People, though, have ever been stubborn in their ways, and so from way back in the early 1700s, they have always called the road General Washington traveled "The King's Highway." It ran all the way from up in Yankee Boston clear down to Rebel Charleston, and it passed right out in front of our brand new church.

Naturally, my Daddy and Mama, and their Bible-believing congregation, named that white brick building with the stained-plastic windows and the blood-red carpet, *The Kingsway Pentecostal Holiness Church.*

And that right there is pure poetry — ask anybody who ever wore baby shoes.

The Kingsway, as it came to be known, was the biggest Pentecostal Holiness Church in all South Carolina. We were told it could hold more people than any other Pentecostal Holiness church in the entire world-wide denomination of Holy Rollers. And, Glory Hallelujah, it was in Myrtle Beach, The Sun Fun City, where we, as God fearing Christians of the Pentecostal Holiness particular, weren't even allowed to go in "mixed-bathing," for the commonly known reason that men and women going swimming together is a Sin. As you might suspect, given the name of the town, right down the road from our new church was a big ol' swimmin' hole, where all kinds of mixed bathing and such goes on — where hot summer fun began on Memorial Day, ended on Labor Day, and lasted almost forever.

Myrtle Beach is what I say when people ask me where I'm from: the small town by the big ocean where I never grew up, where I set records in Dixie Youth Baseball, quit high school football, and got ran out of town by the law before I turned twenty-one.

My Granddaddy called it "Sin City." He said it was perched precarious, on the edge of the briny deep, with the highway to hell winding wide through the middle of it — not straight through the middle because, as Granddaddy explained, "The highway to hell ain't even a little bit straight, nor is there anything narrow about it."

It was where Mama surprised Daddy speechless one Sunday morning when she stole his place behind the pulpit to tell a whole church full of heavenly-minded, behind-her-back-talking, straight-and-narrow people she was taking her babies to the beach to go swimming and that any of the women who wanted to meet her there were invited. Oh, and yes, she would be wearing her bathing suit, like anybody with any sense dresses when they go to the beach.

It is where my Daddy made his mark, as a preacher and a business-man, only to have it washed off by the vodka none of us could smell until it was too late, and that never quite drowned the pain of his baby and her Mama dying before he did.

In those days, most everybody went to church. The doctors, lawyers, accountants, architects and such, along with their wives and children, were Baptists, Methodists, Presbyterians or Lutherans, and even Catho-lics. Like us Pentecostals, they all had church on Sunday mornings, but their worship of God Almighty was structured in such a way as to get Sunday School, singing, and all the preaching over and done with by noon, so as to be home by one o'clock to catch the Sunday kickoff.

The Baptists were nearly as strict as us Pentecostals — no dancin' or drinking and such — but they believed "once saved always saved," and we knew full well even a certified saint could backslide and bust hell wide open if they were to die in their sins before making their way back down to the altar, begging Jesus to forgive them again. And anyways, they regularly made it home from church on Sundays in time for the kickoff, just like all those other half-assed Christians and Catholics. Some of them even smoked.

We Pentecostals knew that weren't no way for a soul to make it past Saint Peter through the Pearly Gate into heaven. On Sundays we almost never got done with the altar call in time to get home for the kickoff, and after a little Shake 'N Bake we were back in Church by six o'clock for the singin' and the sermon, so as to make sure Jesus knew we loved Him way more than wanting to see what happened in the fourth quarter of the National Football League Championship game.

I outgrew my baby shoes years before I began to truly reflect on how yes, Jesus loves me, but I was likely wearing them while learning that little song about being precious in His sight, just like all those little red, yellow and black children who were, most assuredly, nowhere to be seen in our Sunday Morning House of Worship. Jesus had them in His sight, no doubt, but they were precious somewhere else.

They had their own little white shoes too, I reckon.

I started holding onto memories and mementos, such as my baby shoes, for my own self when I went Off To College over in Columbia, at The University of South Carolina. There, I wore shoes that took me into places I wouldn't want to be found if Jesus was to come back, in the twinkling of an eye, to rapture the Saints of God.

On my last day at home, I was in my bedroom packing my clothes to leave when Granddaddy came in to say his goodbyes and pray for me. I remember how he cried, lamenting over how them godless professors were sure to try and fill my head with all kinds of crazy notions that would run the risk of rendering me not so precious in Jesus' sight.

One of those professors made fun of my people and me because of a story I wrote. She assigned an in-class essay, and we wrote about someone who had a significant influence on our lives. She gushed over the homely girl who wrote all forlorn about Sylvia Plath. She read aloud from the essay by the pretty Yankee boy who wrote so tender on Oscar Wilde.

I did not yet know about Sylvia or Oscar, so I wrote about my Granddaddy, the Pentecostal Holiness preacher.

This English professor of creative writing saw fit to read some of my essay to the class. She stopped right in the middle of it to ask if my Grandaddy danced around with rattlesnakes while he was speaking in tongues. I told her, "No Ma'am, we don't hold with no dancin' in our church, but I did see Grandaddy blow a rattlesnake's head off with his twelve-gauge one time."

She probably finished out her tenure over at the University encouraging aspiring young writers to think deep thoughts on important things, like how come e.e. cummings wrote in lower case, and such. She gave me the very first and only "D" I ever got in my whole life. I can't, for the life of me, remember her name.

I reveled in the extended party of Going Off To College, but I didn't last. After a couple of years, I packed my "D" paper in a box with all my other writings of angsty poetry and such, loaded the bed of my Ford pick-up with my Pioneer stereo, all my records, books, and clothes. I laid my old Guild guitar on the seat beside me and headed back down to Myrtle Beach.

I lied to Daddy that I was homesick for him, my sisters and all my friends, and that I would continue college out at Coastal Carolina, which was accredited, and only fifteen minutes out Highway 501 from Myrtle Beach. The real reason I moved back to the beach was so I could play that guitar and sing songs in a bar my friend, Al Hitchcock, had opened. It was called "Drunken Jack's" and it was my first steady paying singing gig.

Playing music in a bar with a name like "Drunken Jack's" got me good and worried about by both my Grandmamas, all my Aunts and Uncles, and good and prayed for by Granddaddy.

Praying is what Granddaddy did better than anybody ever. He and God were old friends who had all sorts of ancient remembrances and understandings between themselves, so when Granddaddy said the blessing before breakfast, dinner or supper, everyone at the table knew he had The Creator's undivided attention. He would ask his old friend, God Almighty, to bless every single person in the family by name, even boyfriends and girlfriends. More than one time he called out some old girlfriends' name with my new girlfriend sitting right there, bless us all.

It went like this: once Grandmama got the biscuits to the table, Granddaddy would look around at all of us until everyone got quiet, then he would close his eyes and pray,

Heavenly Father, we come to You, undeserving, of Your Mercy and Grace, ever mindful of how You sacrificed Your Only Son, Jesus, on a Cross of shame, and mightily raised Him from the dead to save us, sinners, each and all, from the everlasting and eternal torments of Hell.

Thank You Father.

God, I humbly ask that You be with each member of the family. Make Your presence greatly known to them, by Your Holy Spirit.

Be with Lizzy, Marion, Hilda, Chuck, Renee and Sherri... Gladys, Jim, Nancy and Michael... Christine and Larry, Mark and Beth and Eric.

In this, the very hour of their deepest need, richly bless them, shield and protect them, guide and direct them, and comfort them, in that divinely special way that only You know, they need.

Now, as we thank You for the beautiful hands that prepared this meal for us here today, I ask that You bless this food, to our nourishment and strength, that we may all be better equipped in our bodies and minds to be Ambassadors for Your Kingdom, steadfast in your boundless grace, ever watchful and ready to meet our soon-coming Saviour, even Jesus, in Whose Precious Name we pray, Amen and Amen.

Grandaddy's blessings got longer and longer, every time one of us got married or had young'uns of our own. I reckon those blessings are what I miss most every Thanksgiving and Christmas dinner since his passing.

Daddy tried to keep pastoring after Mama died — after God turned a deaf ear to the prayers of the faithful who built The Kingsway — after He surely heard, but did not honor even the prayers of His old friend, my Granddaddy, because He did not take The Cancer away from Mama, but let The Cancer take Mama away from us. After all that, Daddy still preached from time to time, but he only lasted as pastor of The Kingsway a couple more years.

I reckon a Pentecostal Holiness Pulpit ain't nowhere to be struggling with believing.

Mama's last years were my eighth, ninth and tenth. She lived them out in the big new two-story brick house Daddy built for us right behind The Kingsway. The house whose walls heard my sisters' secrets — where I laid me down to sleep and dreamed the dreams that never came quite as true as I dreamed them.

Once Mama died, Daddy moved out of their master bedroom and into the guest room.

Grandaddy left the church he was pastoring so he and Grandmama could move into the master bedroom to take over the stuff Mama used to do. Grandaddy became the assistant pastor at The Kingsway, and ran my sisters and me back and forth to school and such, while Grandmama cooked and cleaned and did the grocery shopping.

It took Daddy nine years, and half that many girlfriends to find the woman who could deal with his peculiar version of crazy. He married Mary while I was off at college, and they, along with my two sisters, were living in that house when I moved back home — back into the house that was re-decorated by my Daddy's new wife.

Mary was good to Daddy; she loved him with all her heart and was with him longer than any of us. Only God knows how. When I moved back in, she had to deal with Renee, Sherri, and now me, in that house still haunted by the ghost of our Mama passed. She did it with uncommon grace, and it could be that even God doesn't know that particular how.

I love Mary. She is one of the finest people I have ever known and I do not say such lightly. But having lived all by myself for two years, there just wasn't any way I could live with all of them in that house, which is how I came to move into the doublewide.

We all knew it was time for me to go. I was just the first to admit it, good and pretty damn loud to Mary, as I was throwing all my belongings into the bed of the Ford F-150 I was driving the morning she told me, "You ain't about to play in some honky-tonk bar all night and then lay up all day long in this house!"

Once Daddy and I had our little say on the matter, I moved into the Fleetwood doublewide, with the sliding-glass door and the cement block deck, situated in a Garden City trailer park a few miles south of where we built that church and a few short feet from the briny deep. There I would live the next four years, between Ocean Boulevard and The King's Highway.

When I unpacked all my never-going-back things for the first time — all my albums: The Beatles, Lightnin' Hopkins, Jethro Tull, The Temptations, James Taylor, Isaac Hayes, and Bob Dylan — my collection of slingshots Granddaddy showed me how to make with the fork of a tree limb, some wire and a bicycle tire inner-tube, my psychedelic posters, black lights, tee-shirts, jeans, bean bag furniture and all the rest. There, at the bottom of a Winn-Dixie cardboard box, I found another, smaller box, with faded gold-stenciled letters.

Somehow, I had managed to hold onto what Mama held onto for me. I pulled this baby shoe, along with the other one from the pair, out of that mess of memories, and set them out on my nightstand, where my girlfriends thought they were cute. They would pick them up and say stuff that usually started with, "Awwww ..."

Those little shoes became a fixture. A familiar. A touchstone. There were times they were tear catchers, looked down into, cradled in hands that were groping for some something to hold onto. Something from back when, back where, me and Mama sang,

Oh victory in Jesus, my saviour forever...

She showed me how I could hold onto the melody while she sang some pretty notes right beside the ones I was singing. Mama called that little bit of beautiful "harmony." She was good at it.

Those little white baby shoes served to remind me of all that and, there on my Coke-crate nightstand, made for a good place to keep my keys.

I sang my song all along that beach town, and started drawing a crowd of people who wanted to hear me sing it. I was making money doing what I loved. I heard my calling and listened to nothing else.

One night my baby sister, Sherri, was coming to see me play a late show. She met a fat and lonely rich boy, head on, from a place called Black Mountain, who had spring-break drunk himself into the north-bound lane of The King's Highway, while going somewhere southward.

You might could say I lost it. You might could say a whole lot of it was already lost.

Less than three months after I refused to look at Sherri in her casket, the powers-that-be in Horry County got their fill of me, and suggested I move far away — they strongly suggested another State. Reluctant and relieved, I obliged them.

I was snow-blind in July, choking on the smoke of a fire I couldn't put out, because what I was pouring on it was feeding the very flames that were burning me down.

The seat I was in was tipping over backwards and I was not holding on, and I was near about to break my fool neck.

I moved to Georgia, went back to college, and in a couple of years picked up a couple of degrees — one in business and one in music. Then I moved to Nashville, Tennessee, to try and be a country music singing star.

I couldn't find those little shoes in any of the boxes I unpacked after moving into the apartment on Magnolia Place, right below an unknown singer named Keith, who turned out to be no stranger to the rain. He ended up saying nothing at all no more forever, proving only that the devil don't give up on nobody — no matter how pretty you sing your song.

Anyhow, Keith Whitley's balcony was right above mine. I heard him singing up there at night, and that's how I figured out I was not a country singer.

I was six hundred miles away from the place I used to call "home," and my little white leather baby shoes were nowhere to be found in any of the wheres I was looking.

I reckon I learned along the way there are some things that just won't bear up under the looking for, because if you really look, long and hard, and you don't find what got lost, it is likely lost for good, in that never-coming-back way.

Sometimes you just get busy looking for other things.

What I found was how life wears it all down smooth, like the Indian's head on the nickel I kept in my pocket for years, because Granddaddy gave it to me and told me he heard tell it was good luck to keep one in your pocket. Then he whispered in my eleven-year-old ear not to let on to any of the church-folk how he said it was good luck. When I asked him how come I couldn't tell, he said, "Son, there's some church people so heavenly-minded, they ain't no earthly good."

And even though I didn't quite know what and all that meant at eleven, I knew enough to know there are some things about being heavenly-minded that ain't worth a nickel's worth of holding onto, much less one with a smoothed down Indian's head on it.

I had it straight from my Granddaddy, who was tight with The Almighty — that same Granddaddy who made sure God remembered to hold onto everyone in the family, by reminding Him of all our first names, whilst saying grace long enough for the coffee and the biscuits and gravy to get cold.

That Indian head nickel is long lost, like back then.

I haven't seen that gold-stenciled box in years, and amongst all its true treasures, it came to hold all my early writings, including the paper with the big red "D" at the top.

I suppose all of it is somewhere out there — somewhere in that grieved place of the lost. That place where even what you hold onto, as tight and tender as you can, will sometimes go.

And then it's just gone.

Gone - like Mama - who never meant to be.

Gone - like Sherri - without even a goodbye.

Gone - like Granddaddy - who knew exactly where he was going.

Gone - like Daddy - even when he was still with us.

Gone - like that other baby-shoe.

Contributors

Marlin Barton lives in Montgomery, Alabama. He's published two novels, *The Cross Garden* and *A Broken Thing*, and two story collections, *The Dry Well* and *Dancing by the River*. He teaches creative writing to juvenile offenders in a program called Writing Our Stories and in the MFA program at Converse College. Find him on Facebook.

Chuck Cannon hails from the South Carolina low-country, a singer-songwriter whose music echoes the R&B, Rock & Roll and Gospel of The South. In addition to his own critically acclaimed recordings, his songs have been covered by mega-stars from around the world, logging nearly 30 million airplays. Follow Chuck on Twitter at @chuckcannon and keep up with his music at chuckcannon.com.

Lisa Carver is a songwriter born in South Carolina and raised in southeast Alaska. Besides touring with her own artist projects, she has had songs cut by other artists including Reba, Sugarland, Julie Roberts, Pam Tillis, Willie Nelson and Tanya Tucker, as well as placed in shows such as *One Life to Live*, *Grey's Anatomy*, and *Army Wives*. Follow Carver on Twitter at @tomwaitswhore.

Chris Clifton was to Texas and music born, known as one of the great guitar stylists playing blues, jazz, rock and country with an artist's soul & a scholar's dedication. He has played, often touring, with some of the best known singer-songwriters in the country, and now makes his home in Fairhope, Alabama, often playing in Key West, Florida.

Cliff Cody, a Texas native, has written songs for such country artists as Julie Roberts, Halfway to Hazard and Josh Thompson. Cliff co-wrote "Down by the River" with D. Vincent Williams, which hit Number 56 on *Billboard Magazine* Hot Country Singles chart. His music can be heard on SiriusXM, IHeart Radio and military radio and live at over 150 gigs he performs each year. He lives in a log cabin in the Appalachian foothills with his wife Amy and daughter Veronica, but spends as much time as possible performing in Key West. Cliff's schedule and more information is available at www.cliffcody.com/ or on Facebook at Cliff Cody band page. Follow Cliff on Twitter at @cliffcodysongs.

Susan Cushman was co-director of the 2013 Oxford Creative Nonfiction Conference and director of the 2011 Memphis Creative Nonfiction Workshop. Her essay, "Chiaroscuro: Shimmer and Shadow" appeared in *Circling Faith: Southern Women on Spirituality* (University of Alabama Press, 2012). She is working on a novel, *Cherry Bomb*. Follow Susan on Twitter at @susancushman. Find Susan on Facebook at sjcushman and at susancushman.com.

Joe Formichella is the prize-winning author of nonfiction works *Here's to you, Jackie Robinson* and *Murder Creek*, among others, and the forthcoming novel *Waffle House Rules*. He currently lives on the Waterhole Branch.

Michael Reno Herrell is a singer-songwriter, a storyteller, a published author, a playwright and speaker. He has performed all across the US and Europe as both musician and storyteller as well as an after dinner and keynote speaker. His writing has been featured in publications such as *Wildlife in North Carolina* and *Storytelling Magazine*. His self-published collection of essays and short stories, *Junk Drawer* is in its fourth printing. Michael has been a featured performer at dozens of music and storytelling festivals including MerleFest and the National Storytelling Festival and has been Teller In Residence at the International Storytelling Center. He leads workshops in both storytelling and songwriting. 2013 marks Michael's fiftieth year as a professional entertainer. His songs have won both gold and platinum awards. He has released thirteen recordings of both music and stories and his CD's have topped the

Americana Music chart. A native of Western North Carolina, much of Michael's material finds its roots in the culture of the Southern Appalachian Mountains. Michael makes his home in Burke County, North Carolina with his wife and manager, Joan, where he is working on his first novel. Learn more about Michael at michaelreno.com on Facebook at michael.r.harrell.7 and listen to his music at www.reverbnation.com/michaelrenoharrell.

Greg Herren is the author of five novels, including *Murder in the Rue St. Ann* and *Mardi Gras Mambo*. He has also edited the anthologies *Shadows of the Night* and *Upon a Midnight Clear*. You can read his ramblings about life, writing, and the world in general at scottynola.com, his webpage at gregherren.com, Facebook at gregherren and on Twitter at @scottynola.

Jennifer Horne is a writer and editor who grew up in Arkansas and has lived for many years in Alabama. She's married to literary critic and interviewer Don Noble, lives by a lake in Cottondale, Alabama, and teaches classes in poetry, memoir, and travel writing for the Honors College at the University of Alabama. Her book *Working the Dirt: An Anthology of Southern Poets* (2003) brought together over one hundred poems about farming and gardening in the South. *Bottle Tree* (2010), a book of poems focusing on Horne's experiences as a Southern woman, was nominated for a SIBA poetry book of the year award. Her two coedited books (with Wendy Reed), *All Out of Faith: Southern Women on Spirituality* (2006) and *Circling Faith: Southern Women on Spirituality* (2012), have received acclaim for the high quality of the essays and their contribution to discussions about religion in the American South. Her collection of short stories, *Tell the World You're a Wildflower*, will be published in the fall 2014 by the University of Alabama Press.

Suzanne Hudson is the prize-winning author of two novels, *In a Temple of Trees* and *In the Dark of the Moon*. Her short fiction has been widely anthologized, and her short story collection, *Opposable Thumbs*, was a finalist for a John Gardner Fiction Book Award. She lives near Fairhope, Alabama.

Michael Knight is the author of two novels, two collections of short stories and a collection of two novellas. He teaches creative writing at the University of Tennessee.

Chuck Jones is a professional songwriter, singer, and guitarist whose songs have been recorded by artists ranging from Patti Labelle, The Fabulous Thunderbirds, and Peter Cetera, to Rascal Flatts, Diamond Rio, Reba McEntire, Kenny Rogers, and Charlie Daniels. He currently resides in Nashville, Tennessee, with his wife and daughter. Follow Chuck on Twitter at @chucksguitar.

Bev Marshall is writer-in-residence at Southeastern Louisiana University and the author of *Walking Through Shadows*, *Right As Rain*, *Hot Fudge Sundae Blues*, and *Shared Words: A Guide to Writers' Groups and Book Clubs*. She lives with her husband in Ponchatoula, Louisiana, where a caged alligator serves as the town's tourist attraction. Find Bev on Facebook at Author Bev Marshall and on her web site at bevmarshall.com.

Janet Nodar. If I could reach back and speak to my eight-year-old self, industriously writing the 1960s version of fanfiction (i.e., my takes on Nancy Drew and the Bobbsey Twins, in pencil in composition books) in my bedroom in San Diego, the one with the plum tree right outside my sliding glass door, I'd say: Well, guess what. When you're fifty four you'll have published some fiction and stuff and now you're a reporter and you've traveled all around the world (and married wisely and had two great kids also, let's not forget) and you wrote a poem about an annual ritual some friends of yours engage in, in which people throw their old shoes into a bonfire as if burning up their sorrows and sins—yes, real shoes, made of leather and rubber and god knows what—and then write and sing about it. And your poem is now part of this story. How cool is that? Pretty cool. Follow Janet on Twitter at @janet_nodar.

Scott Owens. Originally from Greenwood, SC, Scott Owens holds degrees from Ohio University, UNC Charlotte, and UNC Greensboro. He currently lives in Hickory, NC, where he teaches at Catawba Valley Community College, edits *Wild Goose Poetry Review* and *234*, writes for the

Outlook newspaper, and serves as vice-president of the NC Poetry Society. His 11 books have received awards from the Academy of American Poets, the Pushcart Prize Anthology, the Next Generation/Indie Lit Awards, the NC Writers Network, the NC Poetry Society, and the Poetry Society of SC. His newest collection of poems, *Eye of the Beholder*, is due out from Main Street Rag in October. Read more about him on his website at scottowenspoet.com.

Jennifer Paddock is the author of the novels *A Secret Word*, *Point Clear* and *The Weight of Memory*. She received an MA in creative writing from NYU. Her shorter work has appeared in *The North American Review*, *Other Voices*, *Garden and Gun*, and *Mr. Beller's Neighborhood*. Follow Jennifer on Twitter at @jenniferlp92.

Wendy Reed is the author of *An Accidental Memoir: How I Killed Someone and Other Stories* and coeditor of two collections, *Circling Faith* and *All Out of Faith*. She has taught at the University of Alabama, where she produced *Bookmark* and *Discovering Alabama*, for which she received two Emmys. She lives with her husband in Waverly. Follow Wendy on Twitter at @wendyreed66.

Judith Richards is author of six novels. Twice she's earned the Alabama Library Association Award, for *Summer Lightning* and *Too Blue to Fly*. Judith collaborated with her husband, author C. Terry Cline Jr., on every book (his and hers) until his death in May 2013. She lives in Fairhope, Alabama. Follow Judith on Twitter at @judyrchrds, on Facebook at Judith-Richards and on her web site at judithrichards.com.

George Singleton has published five collections of stories, two novels, and a book of writing advice. He teaches at Wofford College in Spartanburg, South Carolina.

Shari Smith has been published in *Thicket Magazine*, *Wildlife in North Carolina*, *Western North Carolina Magazine*, *O.Henry Magazine*, *Pinestraw Magazine*, and *Abilene Living*, and has written for BMI (Broadcast Music Incorporated). Smith authors the blog *Gunpowder, Cowboy Boots, and Mascara* and is working on her first book of nonfiction, *I am a Town*.

Ed Southern is the executive director of the North Carolina Writers' Network. His books include *Parlous Angels, Voices of the American Revolution in the Carolinas*, and *The Jamestown Adventure*. He lives in Winston-Salem. You can find him online at dixiebabble.com.

Lari White's music has earned three Grammys, and RIAA Gold. With her wide range as a singer, songwriter, actress and producer, she has starred on Broadway (*Ring Of Fire*), and graced stages from Carnegie Hall to the Houston Astrodome. Lari turned heads on the silver screen opposite Tom Hanks in *Cast Away*, and made music history as the female producer of Toby Keith's platinum album *White Trash with Money*. Follow Lari on Twitter at @skinnywhitegirl.

North Carolina native **Jim Wilson** is the editor of *Wildlife in North Carolina* magazine, now in its seventy-sixth year of publication. He graduated from the University of North Carolina at Chapel Hill in 1977 with a degree in English. At UNC he studied Southern literature with Louis Rubin and fiction writing with short story writer and novelist Max Steele and poet Jim Seay. He has worked for a variety of publications, including newspapers and magazines, prior to coming to *Wildlife in North Carolina*. Wilson has won numerous national writing awards from the Association for Conservation Information, a peer group for state-agency magazines. Outside of his work, he spends most of his time pursuing trout with a fly rod in the North Carolina mountains, with no great success.

Baynard Woods is the author of *Coffin Point: The Strange Cases of Ed McTeer Witchdoctor Sheriff* and the senior editor of the *Baltimore City Paper*. His work has appeared in *McSweeney's, The Georgia Review*, and the *Millions*. Follow Baynard on Twitter at @baynardwoods.